My First Sound Blends

DK Learning

Produced for DK by WonderLab Group LLC
Designers Project Design Company
Reading Specialist Dr. Jennifer Albro
Illustrated by Rowena Blyth, Chris Cady,
Sarah Corcoran, Sara Lynn Cramb, Sunita Gahir,
Priyal Mote, Gal Weizman, Alisha Monnin
Publisher Sarah Forbes
Publishing Project Manager Katherine Neep
Managing Editor Amelia Jones
Art Director Sarah Corcoran
Publishing Assistant Bryony Brain

First American Edition, 2024
Published in the United States by DK Publishing,
a division of Penguin Random House LLC
1745 Broadway, 20th Floor, New York, NY 10019

A catalog record for this book
is available from the Library of Congress.
ISBN 978-0-5938-4938-5

DK books are available at special discounts when purchased
in bulk for sales promotions, premiums, fund-raising,
or educational use.
For details, contact: DK Publishing Special Markets,
1745 Broadway, 20th Floor, New York, NY 10019
SpecialSales@dk.com

Printed and bound in China

www.dk.com

This book was made with Forest
Stewardship Council™ certified
paper – one small step in DK's
commitment to a sustainable future.
Learn more at
www.dk.com/uk/information/sustainability

Dear Caregivers,

This workbook is organized into eight stages that each focus on sounds made by more than one letter. Stage 1 focuses on the vowel team **ee**. Stages 2 through 7 cover blends (like **cr** in "crust") and digraphs (like **ch** in "chin"). Digraphs have two letters that have only one sound. Stage 8 teaches vowel consonant silent e (like **a-e** in "bake"). In each stage, the child will learn new sounds and practice using them, write words and sentences based on the sounds and spelling rules, read "heart" words (words children learn by heart), and practice comprehension skills.

When the child learns a new sound, have them watch your mouth as you make the sound. Then have the child practice. It is helpful to have them look at their mouth in a mirror as they make the sound so they can see the placement of their mouth, lips, and tongue. When modeling sounds, ensure the child clips the sounds and does not add an /uh/ sound at the end. For example, the /ch/ sound should only be /ch/, not /chuh/, and their mouth should only open slightly.

As the child learns new sound blends, be sure to have them collect the corresponding stickers and add them to the journey map on **pages 6–7.**

As you work with the child, it is important to emphasize the letter(s)–sound relationship consistently. This helps them match the written letter (visual) with its sound (auditory). Some activities start with written letter(s) and ask the child to say the sounds. This is called decoding, or reading. Other activities ask the child to say the word or sounds first and then write or spell the letters. This is called encoding, or spelling.

In each stage, the child will practice reading and spelling "heart" words. Heart words have regular and irregular parts. The child can sound out the regular parts because they make the sound the child has learned. For example, the **d** in the word "does" makes the /d/ sound. The child will need help reading the irregular parts because they do not follow the sounds they have learned. In the same example, the **oe** in "does" makes the /u/ sound and the **s** makes the /z/ sound. As the child reads and spells heart words, ensure that they know the irregular parts and that they "learn them by heart."

were

- Sound buttons are used to help identify individual sounds in words. Dots are used to show separate sounds. Lines are used under two or more letters that represent one sound.

- Hearts are used to identify the tricky part of the word that must be "learned by heart."

In Stage 7, some of the words are coded by syllable instead of by sound. Each word has one arrow and individual lines within the arrow to show each syllable. Encourage the child to read each syllable and then blend them to read the whole word. Example: run + ning = running.

Lastly, look for the "Tips" for suggestions on blending sounds, modeling mouth formations when making sounds, teaching spelling rules, and games that practice phonics skills.

Happy Reading!

Contents

Sound Blends Journey Map

As you learn new sound blends, collect the corresponding stickers and add them to this map.

CCVC

CVCC

STAGE 1

ee

ch

sh

th

STAGE 3

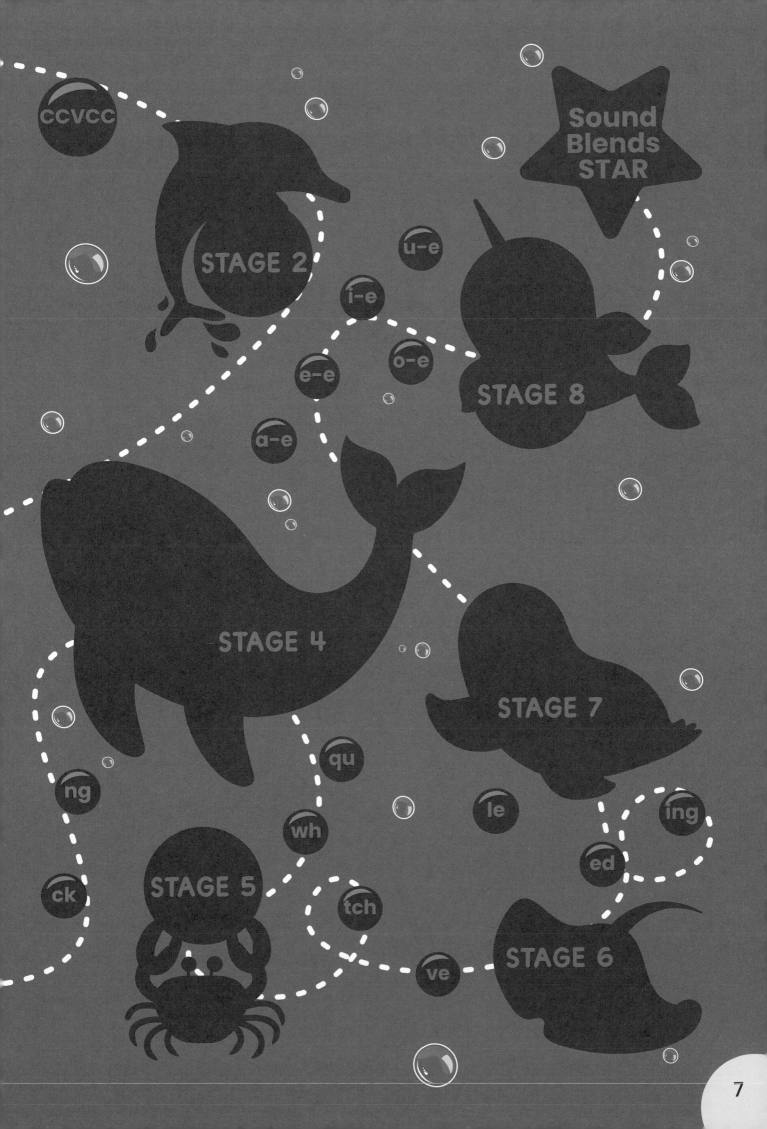

CCVCC

STAGE 2

Sound
Blends
STAR

u-e

i-e

e-e

o-e

STAGE 8

a-e

STAGE 4

STAGE 7

qu

ng

wh

le

ing

ed

ck

STAGE 5

tch

STAGE 6

ve

ee

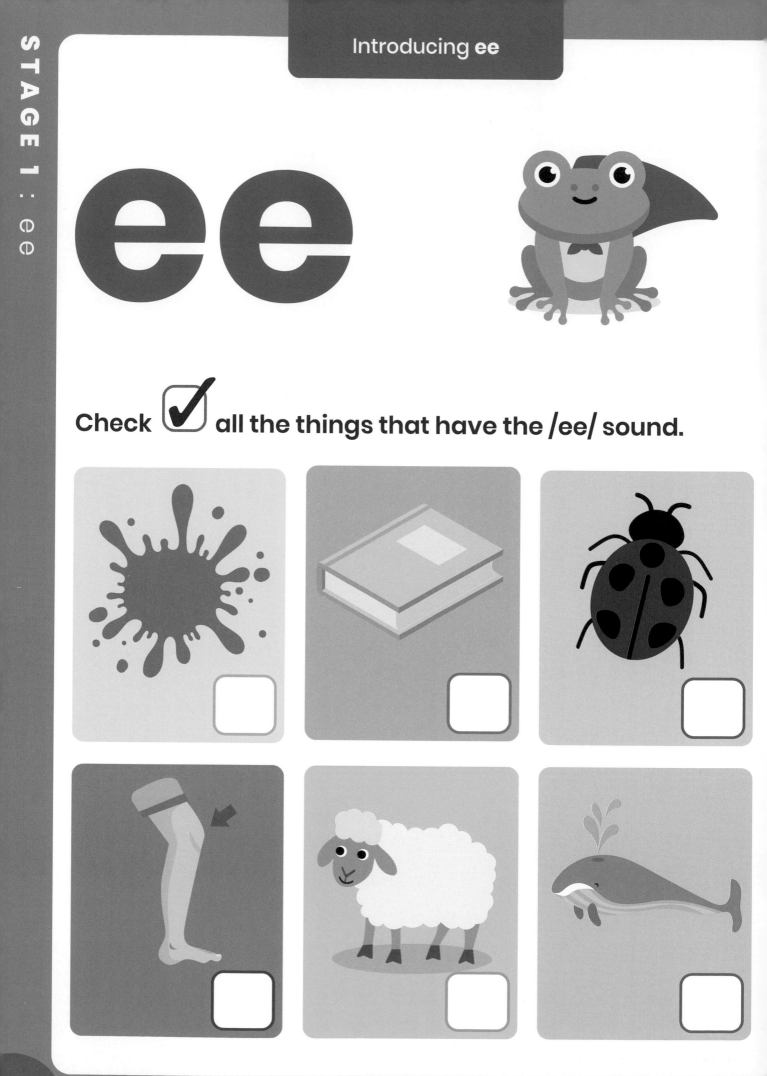

Check ✔️ all the things that have the /ee/ sound.

Color all the things that have the /ee/ sound.

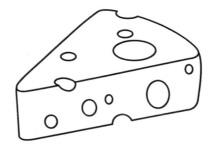

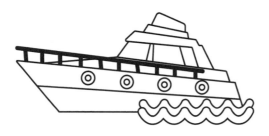

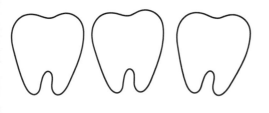

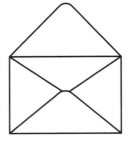

The /ee/ sound

Circle the thing in each row that has the /ee/ sound.

The /ee/ sound

Look at these words and pictures. Say the words and match them to the pictures.

tree   **seed**   **feed**   **beep**

sleep   **feet**   **see**   **bee**

Look at these words. Blend the sounds to read the whole word.

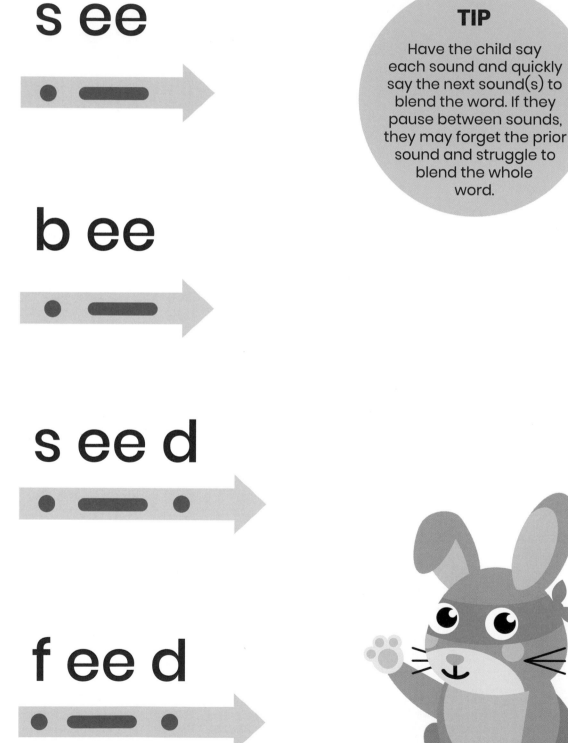

s ee

b ee

s ee d

f ee d

TIP

Have the child say each sound and quickly say the next sound(s) to blend the word. If they pause between sounds, they may forget the prior sound and struggle to blend the whole word.

Blend the sounds in each square to read the whole word.

t	r	ee

b	ee	p

f	ee	t

s	l	ee	p

Trace the word.

bee   bee   bee

Copy the word.

Trace the word.

tree   tree   tree

Copy the word.

Trace the word.

feet   feet   feet

Copy the word.

Trace the word.

green   green

Copy the word.

Congratulations!

Now you know your **ee** sound.

Well done!

Collect an animal sticker to add to your journey map.

STAGE 1 COMPLETE

Have you collected all of your sound blend bubbles from the sticker page?

Read the words in the box. Color the pictures that match the words in the box.

| bank | belt | bugs | cats | cubs |

gift   hand   jump   lamp   tent

Look at these words. Blend the sounds to read the whole word.

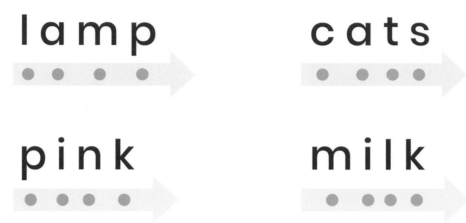

l a m p

c a t s

p i n k

m i l k

Look at these words and pictures. Say the words and match them to the pictures.

hand   gift   tent   bump

pink   milk   cats   lamp

Blend the sounds in each square to read the whole word.

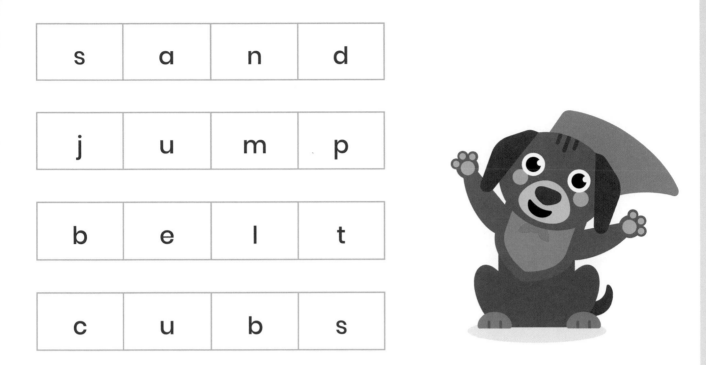

| s | a | n | d |

| j | u | m | p |

| b | e | l | t |

| c | u | b | s |

Write the words from above next to the correct picture.

___ ___ ___ ___

___ ___ ___ ___

___ ___ ___ ___

___ ___ ___ ___

STAGE 2 : CVCC

Fill in the first missing sound. Blend the sounds to read the whole word.

___ ank

___ amp

___ ind

___ ink

___ ugs

___ ats

Fill in the second missing sound. Blend the sounds to read the whole word.

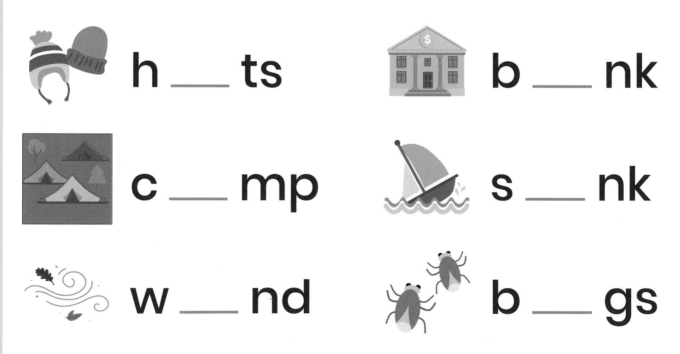

h ___ ts

b ___ nk

c ___ mp

s ___ nk

w ___ nd

b ___ gs

Fill in the third missing sound. Blend the sounds to read the whole word.

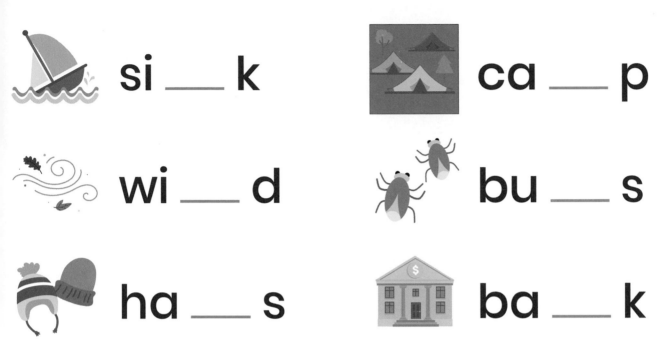

si __ k   ca __ p

wi __ d   bu __ s

ha __ s   ba __ k

Fill in the final missing sound. Blend the sounds to read the whole word.

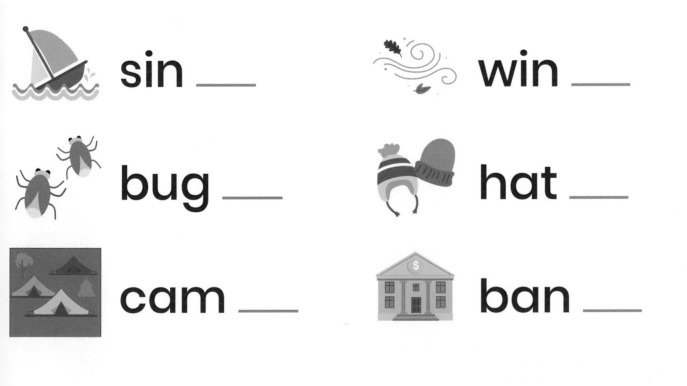

sin __   win __

bug __   hat __

cam __   ban __

Heart words

Read the heart words.

were

here

there

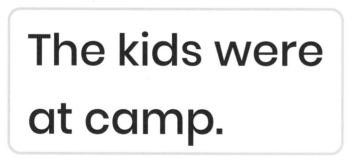

Read the sentences. Match each sentence to the correct picture.

The kids were at camp.

Here is a nest.

A cliff is up there.

Copy the heart words.

were

here

there

Write the heart words to complete the sentences.

The belt and the hats

_____ left in the tent.

_____ is the dent.

Now the lamp is bent.

Where is the desk?

It is _____ .

Read the sentences. Circle the correct word to complete each sentence.

Bob's bag is
pink / red .

There were bugs
in the tent / bag .

The milk / lamp
is here.

Read the sentences. Find the sticker for each sentence on the sticker page.

Bob and Lin got to the damp camp.

Bob lost the lamp. "Where is it?"

Lin fell off the log with a bump. "Jump, Bob!"

"The tent is there!" said Lin.

Writing sentences

Trace the sentence.

Bob and Lin got to the damp camp.

Trace the sentence.

Bob lost the lamp. "Where is it?"

Trace the sentence.

Lin fell off the log with a bump. "Jump, Bob!"

Trace the sentence.

"The tent is there!" said Lin.

Camp game

For 1 to 4 players. You will need tokens and a die. Take turns throwing the die and moving your token. Read the word you land on. If you land on a rock, you miss a turn. The winner is the first person to the tent!

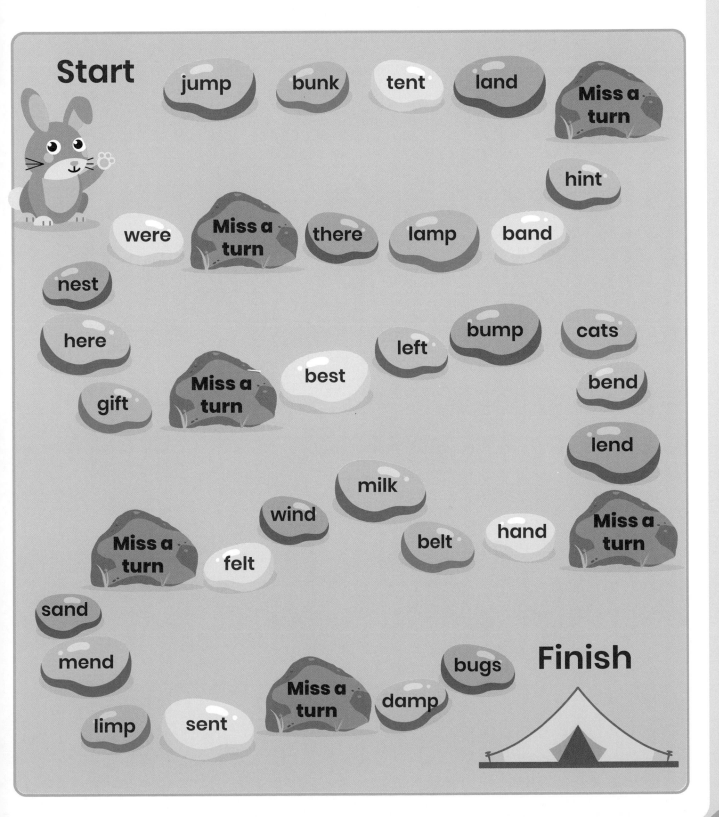

Here are 15 things that each have four sounds.
Which of these things can you find in the big picture?

Check ☑ the things you find.

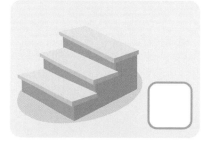

Look at these words. Blend the sounds to read the whole word.

f r o g

f l i p

p l u m

c l a p

Look at these words and pictures. Circle the two words that do not have a matching picture.

plum	snap	frog	clap
flip	grab	step	trim

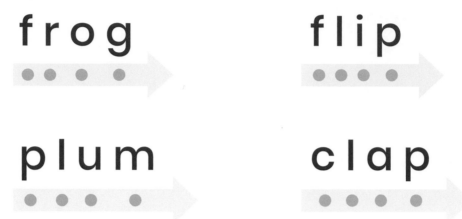

Blend the sounds in each square to read the whole word.

| t | w | i | g |

| f | l | a | g |

| s | l | e | d |

| g | r | i | n |

Write the words from above next to the correct picture.

____ ____ ____ ____

____ ____ ____ ____

____ ____ ____ ____

____ ____ ____ ____

Fill in the first missing sound. Blend the sounds to read the whole word.

___ rab

___ rum

___ wim

___ kip

___ rin

___ lip

Fill in the second missing sound. Blend the sounds to read the whole word.

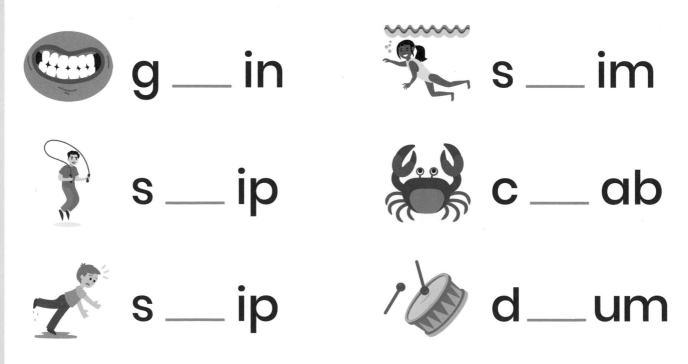

g ___ in

s ___ im

s ___ ip

c ___ ab

s ___ ip

d ___ um

Fill in the third missing sound. Blend the sounds to read the whole word.

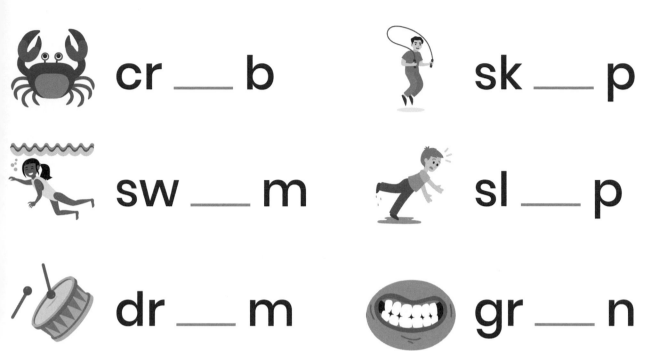

cr __ b   sk __ p

sw __ m   sl __ p

dr __ m   gr __ n

Fill in the final missing sound. Blend the sounds to read the whole word.

sli __   dru __

swi __   gri __

ski __   cra __

Read the heart words.

two

he

she

Read the sentences. Match each sentence to the correct picture.

Two cats slept on a mat.

He can jump up and flip.

She will skip and trip!

Copy the heart words.

two _____

he _____

she _____

Write the heart words to complete the sentences.

What is one plus one?
It is _____ .

Jen said _____ had a plan.

The man said _____ was lost.

Read the sentences. Circle the correct word to complete each sentence.

The crab can snap / drum the twig.

Fran is glum / grin .

The spin / sled is at the top of the hill.

Read the sentences. Match each sentence to a picture.

Fran the frog will sled and Bret the dog will run. Will Fran win?
Will Bret win?

Fran's sled slid from the top of the hill.
"I will win!" yells Fran.

Fran gets to the flag.
"Huff! Puff!" says Bret.

Bret and Fran clap and grin. "It was so fun!"

Trace the sentence.

Fran will sled and
Bret will run.

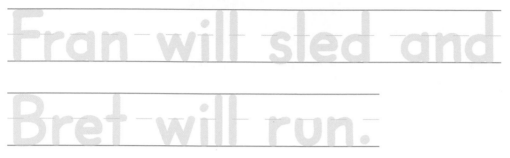

Trace the sentence.

Fran's sled slid from
the top of the hill.

Trace the sentence.

Fran gets to the flag.
"Huff! Puff!" says Bret.

Trace the sentence.

Bret and Fran clap and
grin. "It was so fun!"

Three-in-a-row game

For 2 players. You will need a die and some tokens. Take turns throwing the die. Read a word in that column and place your token on that word. The first player to have three tokens in a row in any direction is the winner!

swim	drum	clap	stop	slid	two
he	brag	Fred	drop	snap	spin
glum	frog	sled	prod	flag	from
flap	she	brim	grin	flop	stun
blob	twin	glad	snip	stem	flip
grin	drip	drag	grit	grab	plum

Color the **spots** on the insects.

Draw a line between the picture in the circle and the one that rhymes with it.

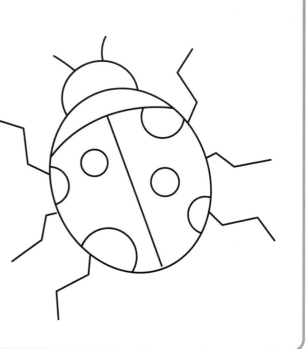

Check ✔ the picture that rhymes with the one in the circle.

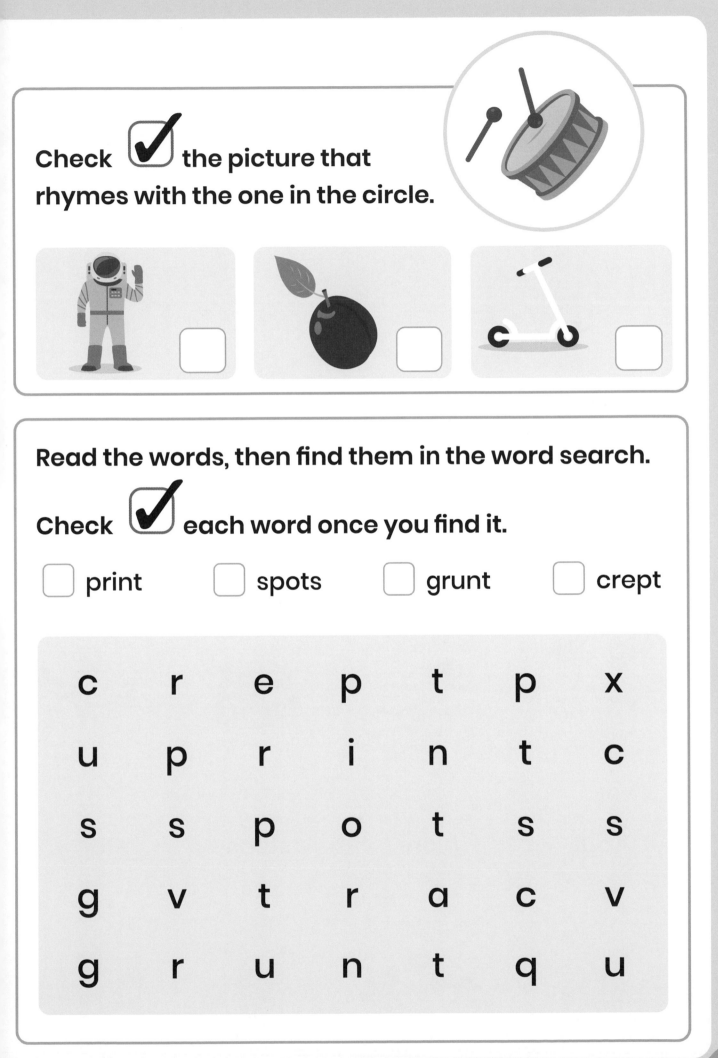

Read the words, then find them in the word search.

Check ✔ each word once you find it.

☐ print   ☐ spots   ☐ grunt   ☐ crept

c	r	e	p	t	p	x
u	p	r	i	n	t	c
s	s	p	o	t	s	s
g	v	t	r	a	c	v
g	r	u	n	t	q	u

Look at these words. Blend the sounds to read the whole word.

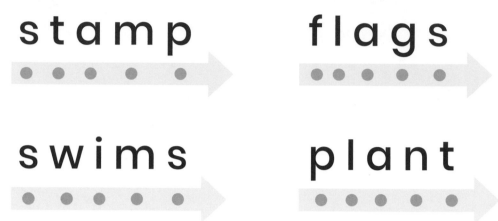

s t a m p

f l a g s

s w i m s

p l a n t

Look at these words and pictures. Say the words and match them to the pictures.

swims   flags   crust   stump

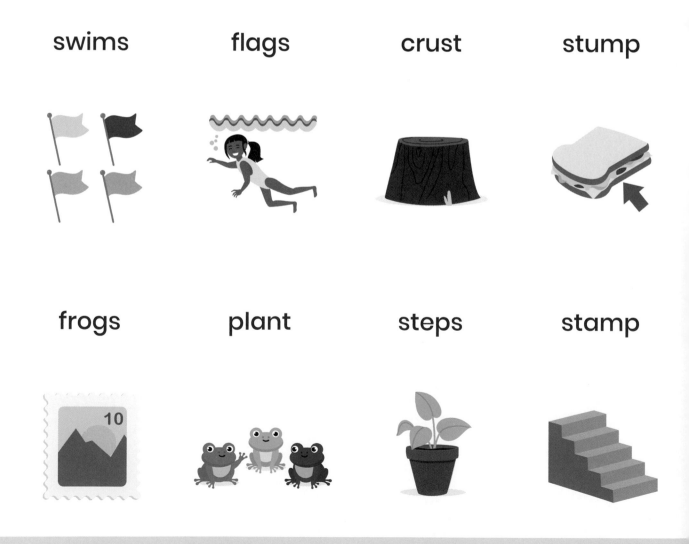

frogs   plant   steps   stamp

Sounding out and blending: CCVCC words

Blend the sounds in each square to read the whole word.

d	r	i	n	k

s	t	o	m	p

f	r	o	s	t

s	t	u	n	t

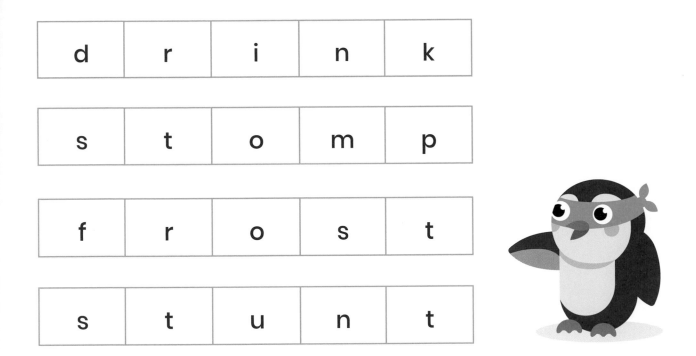

Write the words from above next to the correct picture.

_____ _____ _____ _____ _____

_____ _____ _____ _____ _____

_____ _____ _____ _____ _____

_____ _____ _____ _____ _____

Fill in the first missing sound. Blend the sounds to read the whole word.

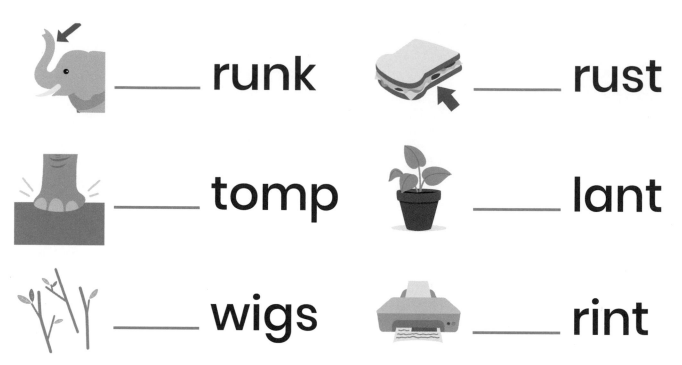

_____ runk

_____ rust

_____ tomp

_____ lant

_____ wigs

_____ rint

Fill in the second missing sound. Blend the sounds to read the whole word.

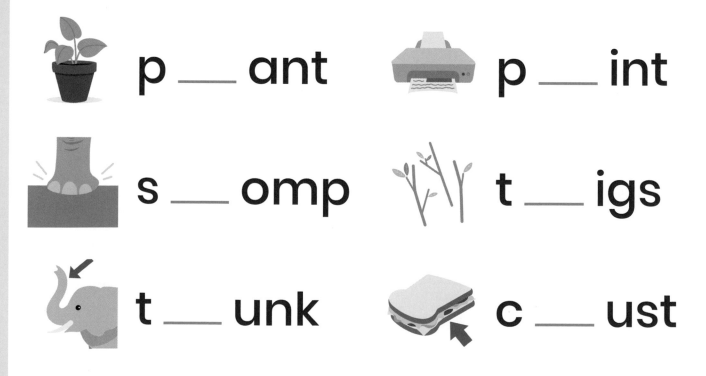

p ___ ant

p ___ int

s ___ omp

t ___ igs

t ___ unk

c ___ ust

Fill in the third missing sound. Blend the sounds to read the whole word.

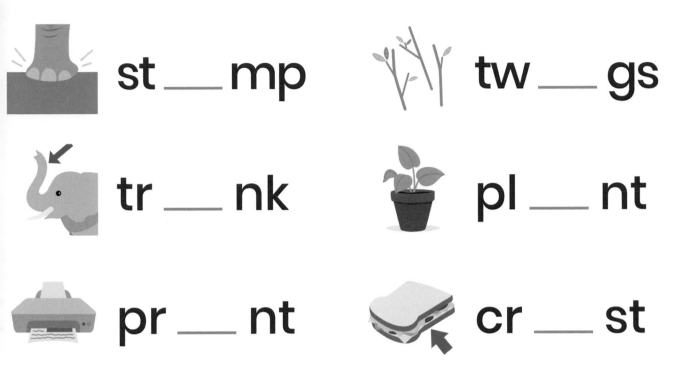

st __ mp   tw __ gs

tr __ nk   pl __ nt

pr __ nt   cr __ st

Fill in the fourth missing sound. Blend the sounds to read the whole word.

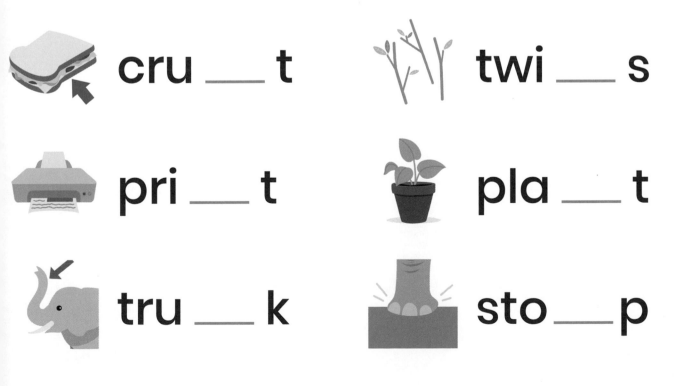

cru __ t   twi __ s

pri __ t   pla __ t

tru __ k   sto __ p

Read the heart words.

we
● ♥

be
● ♥

me
● ♥

Read the sentences. Match each sentence to the correct picture.

We slept in a tent.

There will be frost on the twigs.

Tess yells to me.

Copy the heart words.

we _____

be _____

me _____

Write the heart words to complete the sentences.

_____ stop to rest and have a drink.

Can a crab _____ a pet?

Mom tells _____ to go to bed.

Read the sentences. Circle the correct word to complete each sentence.

She **drank / skips** the milk.

The dog ran to **we / me** .

Can we **are / be** pals?

Read the poem out loud.

Lin and Alf run past the tree.

Alf stomps for all to see!

He has a trunk and tusks.

Alf sees that it is dusk.

Lin trips on the stump!

Did Alf slip or did he jump?

Draw a picture of your favorite part of the poem.

Trace the sentence.

Alf stomps for all to see.

Trace the sentence.

He has a trunk and tusks.

Trace the sentence.

Lin trips on the stump!

Trace the sentence.

Did Alf slip or did he jump?

Congratulations!

Now you know your CCVC, CVCC, and CCVCC words.

Well done!

Collect an animal sticker to add to your journey map.

STAGE 2 COMPLETE

Have you collected all of your sound blend bubbles from the sticker page?

CVCC

CCVCC

CCVC

ch words

Look at these words. Blend the sounds to read the whole word.

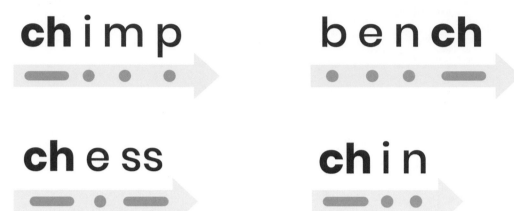

ch i m p

b e n **ch**

ch e ss

ch i n

Look at these words and pictures. Circle the two words that do not have a matching picture.

chess	bench	lunchbox	chest
sandwich	chimp	pinch	chin

TIP

Model the /ch/ sound. Say, "My tongue is touching my top side teeth, with the tip on the roof of my mouth. I push air and stop right before letting it out. I don't use my voice."

Blend the sounds in each square to read the whole word.

ch	o	p

l	u	n	ch

ch	ee	k

ch	a	t

Write the words from above next to the correct picture.

_____ _____ _____

_____ _____ _____ _____

_____ _____ _____

_____ _____ _____

Look at these words. Blend the sounds to read the whole word.

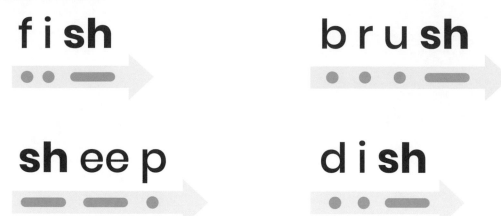

f i **sh**

b r u **sh**

sh ee p

d i **sh**

Find the sticker for each word on the sticker page, and stick it on the matching word below.

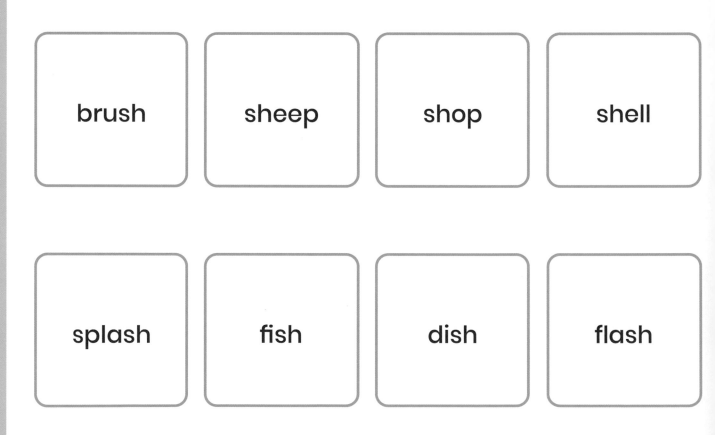

| brush | sheep | shop | shell |

| splash | fish | dish | flash |

Blend the sounds in each square to read the whole word.

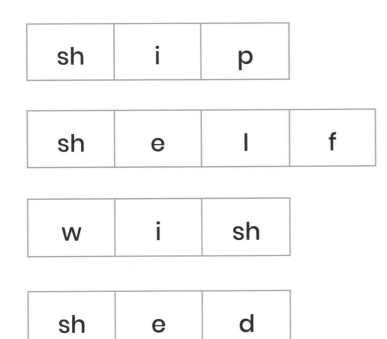

sh	i	p	

sh	e	l	f

w	i	sh	

sh	e	d	

Write the words from above next to the correct picture.

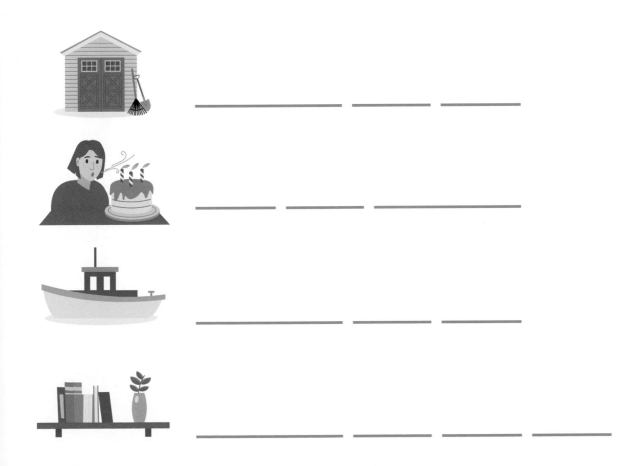

Look at these words. Blend the sounds to read the whole word.

m o **th**

t ee **th**

th e n

th a n k s

Color each shape with a thing that has the /th/ sound.

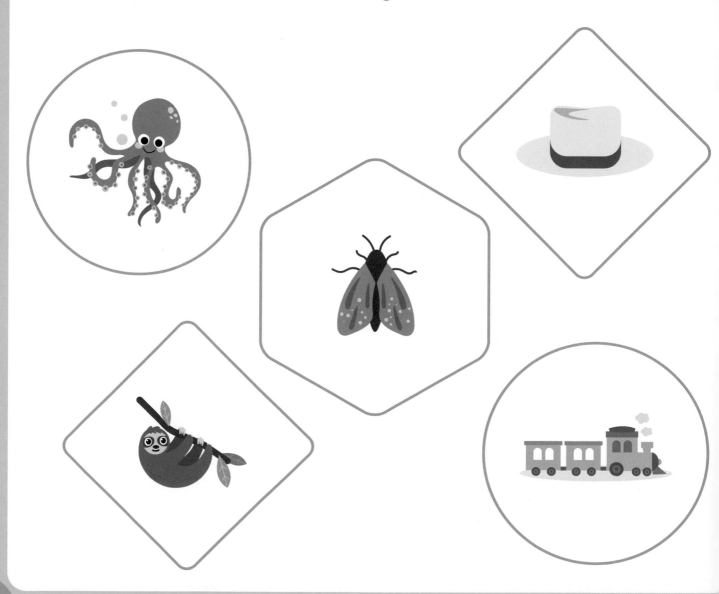

Blend the sounds in each square to read the whole word.

f	i	f	th

th	i	n	k

c	l	o	th

th	r	ee

Write the words from above next to the correct picture.

_____ _____ _____ _____

_____ _____ _____

_____ __ _____ _____

_____ _____ _____

Sorting **ch sh th**

Here are 10 things that have the /ch/, /sh/, or /th/ sound. Which of these things can you find in the big picture?

Check ✔ the things you find.

Color each section that has a thing that has the /ch/, /sh/, or /th/ sound.

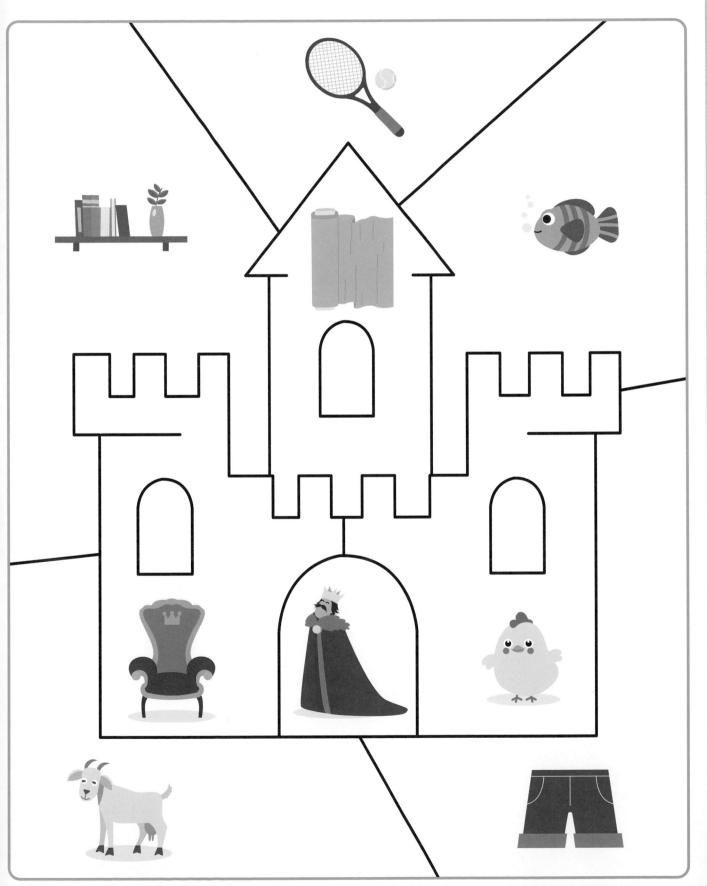

Fill in the first missing sound. Blend the sounds to read the whole word.

___ ench

___ imp

___ elf

___ rush

___ ifth

___ ixth

Fill in the second missing sound. Blend the sounds to read the whole word.

b ___ ush

s ___ xth

ch ___ mp

f ___ fth

b ___ nch

sh ___ lf

TIP

Have the child say the picture's name and then hold up a finger for each sound in the word. Ask, "What's the missing sound?" Then have them write the missing sound.

Fill in the third missing sound. Blend the sounds to read the whole word.

she __ f

si __ th

be __ ch

chi __ p

fi __ th

br __ sh

Fill in the final missing sound. Blend the sounds to read the whole word.

fif __

bru __

shel __

ben __

chim __

six __

Read the heart words.

they

their

who

Read the sentences. Match each sentence to the correct picture.

They crunch and munch.	
Their job was to dig a trench.	
Who is there?	

Copy the heart words.

they _____

their _____

who _____

Write the heart words to complete the sentences.

_____ are chums.

The twins lost _____ lunchbox.

_____ let the cat out?

Read the sentences. Circle the correct word to complete each sentence.

This is **they / their** ship.

I have six eggs.
This is the **sixth / tenth** .

Froth / Thank you for the gift.

Read the sentence.

Three chimp chums chit chat on three trees.

Color the chimp.

TIP

After reading these tongue twisters, have the child try to come up with their own using either /sh/, /ch/, or /th/. Write them down to practice reading them.

Read the sentence.

Sloths sleep, moths munch the cloth, and the bees buzz, buzz, buzz.

Circle the sloth, moth, and cloth.

Read the sentence, then draw Shell the fish.

Shell the fish flips and flops off the ship and swims off with a swish. Splish! Splash!

Trace the sentence.

The three chimps
are chums.

Trace the sentence.

Moths munch
the cloth.

Trace the sentence.

Shell the fish flips and
flops off the ship.

Trace the sentence.

Six sheep skip in
the shed.

Congratulations!

Now you know your **ch**, **sh**, and **th** sounds.

Well done!

Collect an animal sticker to add to your journey map.

STAGE 3 COMPLETE

Have you collected all of your sound blend bubbles from the sticker page?

ch

sh

th

Look at these words. Blend the sounds to read the whole word.

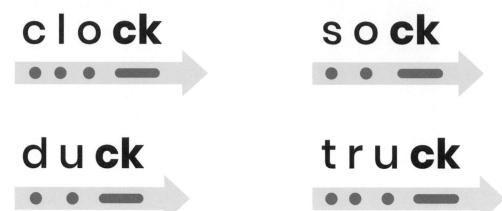

c l o **ck**

s o **ck**

d u **ck**

t r u **ck**

Look at these words and pictures. Say the words and match them to the pictures.

duck   snack   rock   truck

backpack   stick   clock   sock

Blend the sounds in each square to read the whole word.

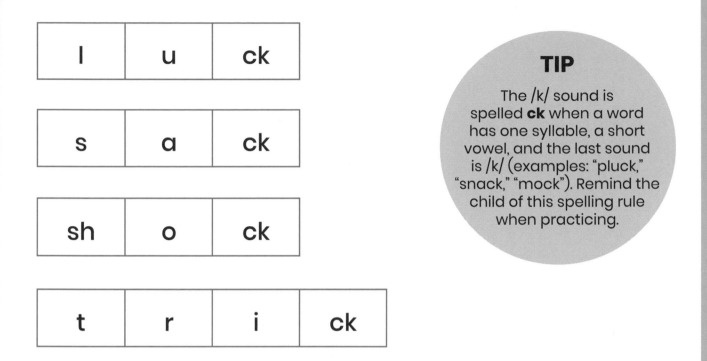

l	u	ck

s	a	ck

sh	o	ck

t	r	i	ck

TIP

The /k/ sound is spelled **ck** when a word has one syllable, a short vowel, and the last sound is /k/ (examples: "pluck," "snack," "mock"). Remind the child of this spelling rule when practicing.

Write the words from above next to the correct picture.

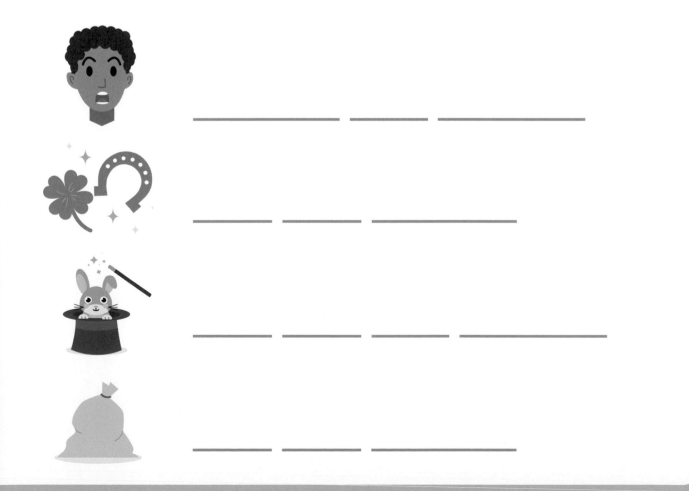

_____ ____ _____

_____ _____ _____

_____ ____ _____ _____

_____ ____ _____

Look at these words. Blend the sounds to read the whole word.

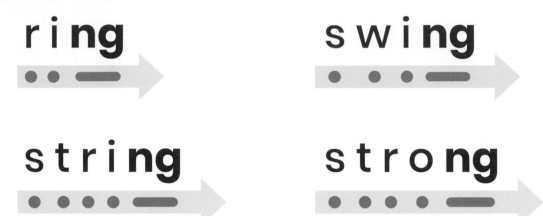

r i **ng**

s w i **ng**

s t r i **ng**

s t r o **ng**

Circle the picture that does not rhyme with the others.

king   swing   sing   long

Circle the picture that does not rhyme with the others.

wing   strong   sting   ring

Blend the sounds in each square to read the whole word.

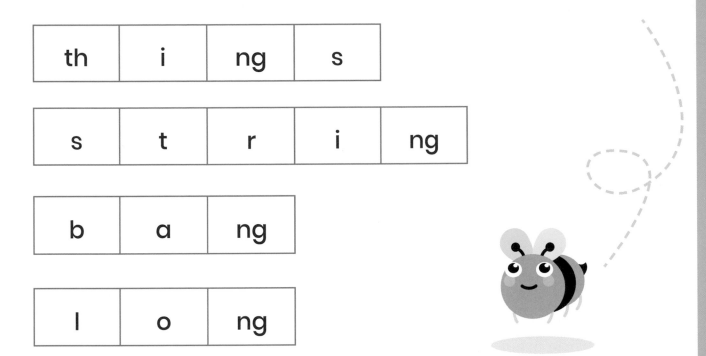

| th | i | ng | s |

| s | t | r | i | ng |

| b | a | ng |

| l | o | ng |

Write the words from above next to the correct picture.

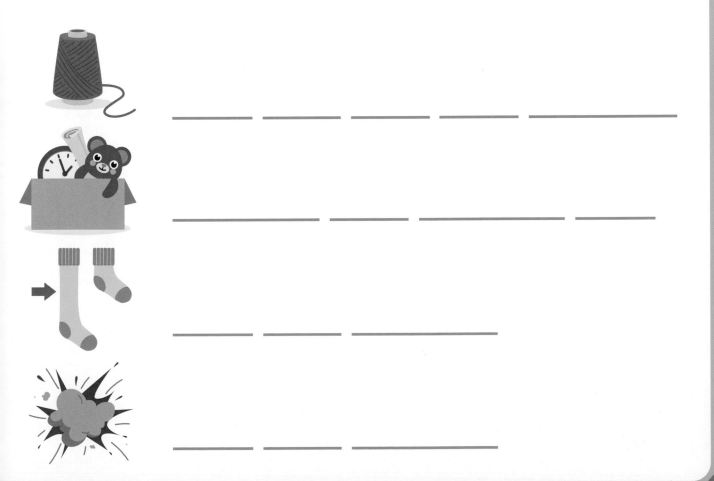

_____ _____ _____ _____

_____ _____ _____ _____

_____ _____ _____

_____ _____

Sorting **ck ng**

Here are 10 things that end with **ck** or **ng**. Which of these can you find in the big picture?

Check ✔️ the things you find.

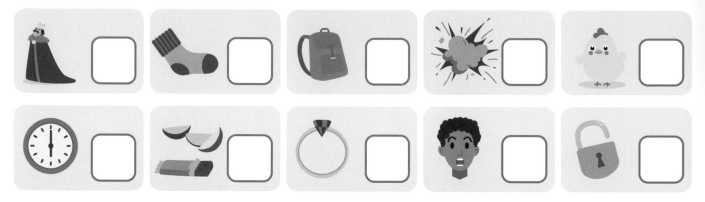

Color each section of the train that has a thing with **ck** or **ng** in it.

TIP

Remind the child that **ck** and **ng** will never be at the beginning of a word, so they need to listen for the last sound after saying the picture's name.

Fill in the first missing sound. Blend the sounds to read the whole word.

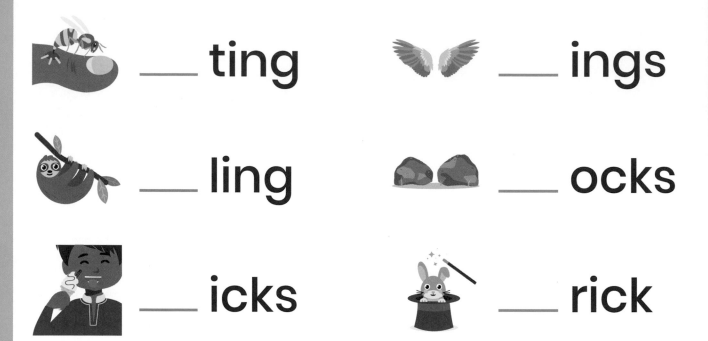

___ ting   ___ ings

___ ling   ___ ocks

___ icks   ___ rick

Fill in the second missing sound. Blend the sounds to read the whole word.

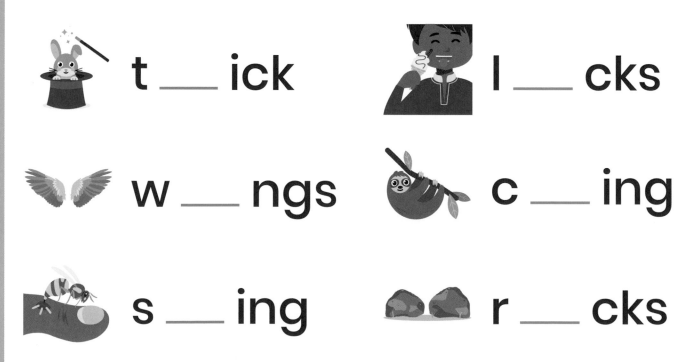

t ___ ick   l ___ cks

w ___ ngs   c ___ ing

s ___ ing   r ___ cks

Fill in the third missing sound. Blend the sounds to read the whole word.

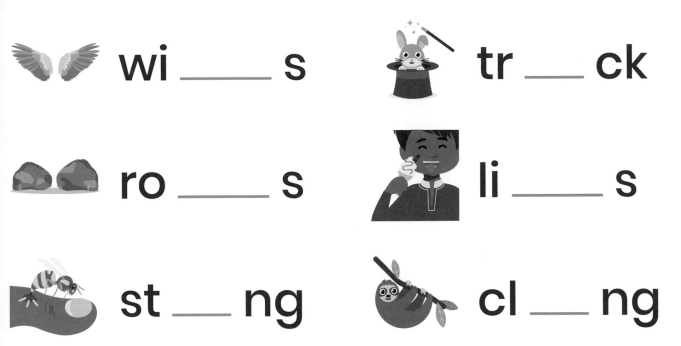

wi ___ s   tr ___ ck

ro ___ s   li ___ s

st ___ ng   cl ___ ng

Fill in the final missing sound. Blend the sounds to read the whole word.

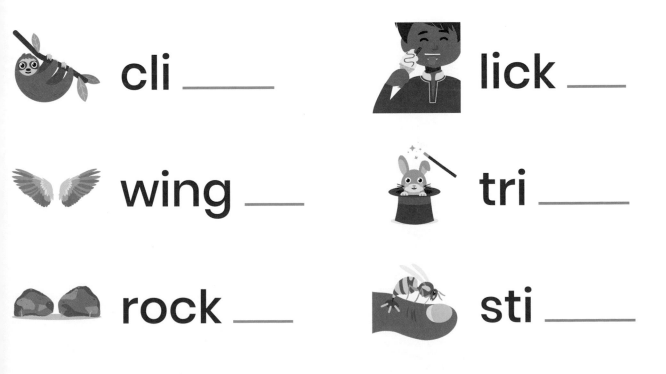

cli ___   lick ___

wing ___   tri ___

rock ___   sti ___

Read the heart words.

my

by

you

Read the sentences. Match each sentence to the correct picture.

My socks are red.

The ducks are by the pond.

You and I sing songs.

Copy the heart words.

my _____

by _____

you _____

Write the heart words to complete the sentences.

_____ dad had a long trip.

The swings are _____

the shed.

Can _____ bring snacks?

STAGE 4 : ck ng

Read the sentences. Circle the correct word to finish each sentence.

This is **you / my** swing.

Do I need to **pack / cling** for the trip?

TIP

Have the child read the sentence with the first word. Example: "This is you swing." Have them read the sentence again with the second word. Example: "This is my swing." Ask, "Which one makes sense?"

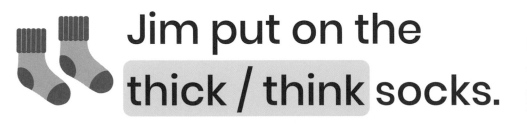

Jim put on the **thick / think** socks.

78

Read the sentences. Match each sentence to the correct picture.

"When can I get on the swing?" says Frank.

"You can get on at six," says Jim.

Tick, tock. It is ten. Frank is mad and bangs the swing.

"Bad luck, Frank!" says Jim. "Let's get back to the camp."

Writing sentences

Trace the sentence.

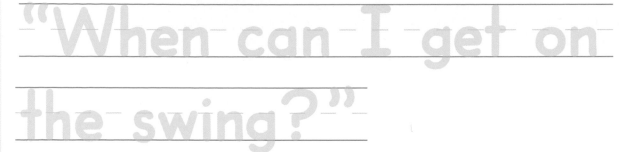

"When can I get on
the swing?"

Trace the sentence.

"You can get on
at six."

Trace the sentence.

Frank is mad and
bangs the swing.

Trace the sentence.

"Bad luck, Frank!"
says Jim.

Congratulations!

Now you know your **ck** and **ng** spellings.

Well done!

Collect an animal sticker to add to your journey map.

STAGE 4 COMPLETE

Have you collected all of your sound blend bubbles from the sticker page?

ck

ng

Color the picture of the **qu**een.

Color the picture of **Qu**in the penguin.

Circle the animal that is **qu**ick.

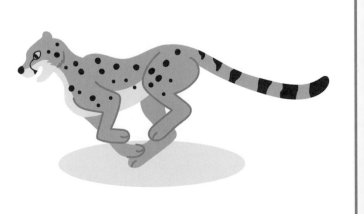

Blend the sounds in each square to read the whole word.

qu	ee	n

qu	i	z

qu	i	ck

Qu	i	n

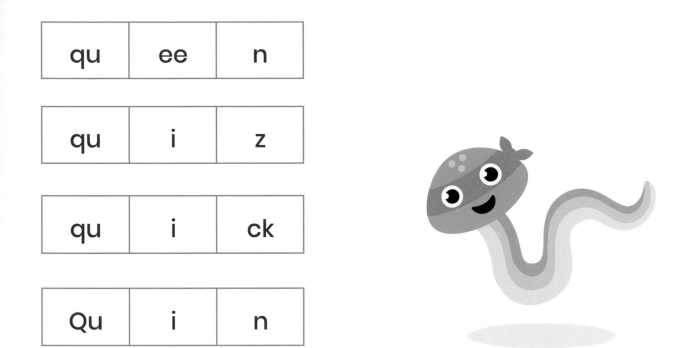

Write the words from above next to the correct picture.

_____ _____ _____

_____ _____ _____

_____ _____ _____

_____ _____ _____

wh words

Check ✔ all the things that start with **wh**.

Blend the sounds in each square to read the whole word.

wh	ee	l

wh	i	ff

wh	a	ck

wh	i	s	k

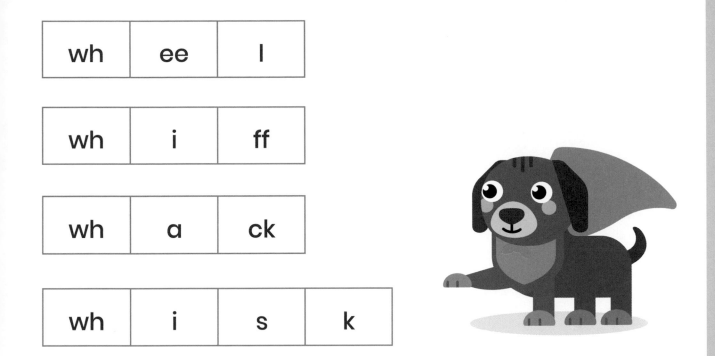

Write the words from above next to the correct picture.

_____ _____ ____ _____

_____ ____ ___

_____ ____ ____

_____ ____ ___

Help Quin find dinner by following the path of all of the real **qu** words.

TIP

Remind the child that **qu** has two sounds: /k/ and /w/. Before starting this activity, practice saying words with the /k/ and /w/ sounds spelled with **qu**.

qualg

quot

quest

queen

quiz

quick

queb

quit

quish

Real and nonsense wh words

Pam is flying a jet. Color each cloud that has a real **wh** word.

whack

whud

whib

wheel

wheff

which

whip

whob

Fill in the missing sound. Blend the sounds to read the whole word. Match the word to the correct picture.

_____ a c k

_____ e e n

_____ i n

_____ i l t

TIP

Have the child say the picture's name first. Ask, "What are the first two sounds you hear?" (Answer: /k//w/) Ask, "What makes those sounds?" Then have them write the missing sounds.

Fill in the missing sound. Blend the sounds to read the whole word. Then color the picture.

_____ i s k

_____ i ff

_____ ee l

Read the heart words.

your
do

does

Read the sentences. Match each sentence with the correct picture.

| Where is your quilt? |

| Do you have a whisk? |

| My mom does a quiz. |

Copy the heart words.

your _____

do _____

does _____

Write the heart words to complete the sentences.

_____ wheel is flat.

Can you _____ a quick trick?

What _____ a queen do?

Read the sentences. Circle the correct word to complete each sentence.

 **Do / Does** Bob need a drink?

 Pick up **your / you** socks.

 This cat is **quack / quick** .

Read the sentences. Match the sentence to the correct picture.

"Where is Lin?" asks Fran.

"Which path should I hop up?" asks Fran.

"Here I am. Quick! I will get up the hill!" says Lin.

"I win! I am the queen of the hill!" says Fran.

TIP

Ask questions about the story to deepen comprehension. Ask, "Can you number the pictures in order of how they happened?" "Who got up the hill first?"

Writing sentences

Trace the sentence.

"Where is Lin?"

asks Fran.

Trace the sentence.

"Which path should

I hop up?"

Trace the sentence.

"Quick! I will get up

the hill!"

Trace the sentence.

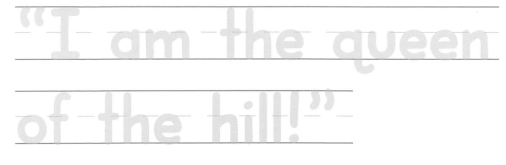

"I am the queen

of the hill!"

Congratulations!

Now you know your **qu** and **wh** spellings.

Well done!

Collect an animal sticker to add to your journey map.

STAGE 5
COMPLETE

Have you collected all of your sound blend bubbles from the sticker page?

qu

wh

tch words

Look at these words. Blend the sounds to read the whole word.

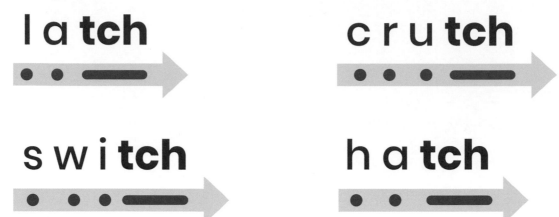

l a **tch**

c r u **tch**

s w i **tch**

h a **tch**

Look at these words and pictures. Say the words and match them with the pictures.

TIP

Tell the child that **tch** spells the /ch/ sound when there's a short vowel before it. After they read the **tch** words, ask them to identify the vowel sound to reinforce the spelling rule.

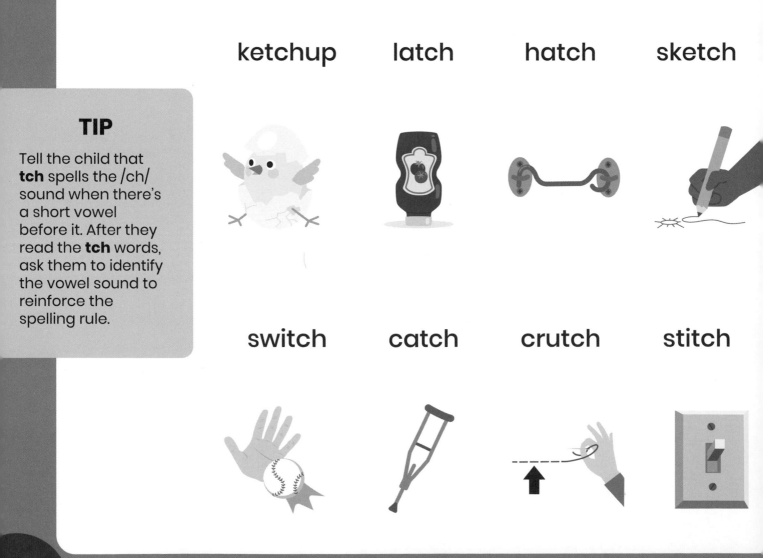

ketchup   latch   hatch   sketch

switch   catch   crutch   stitch

Blend the sounds in each square to read the whole word.

| f | e | tch |

| d | i | tch |

| s | t | r | e | tch |

| s | c | r | a | tch |

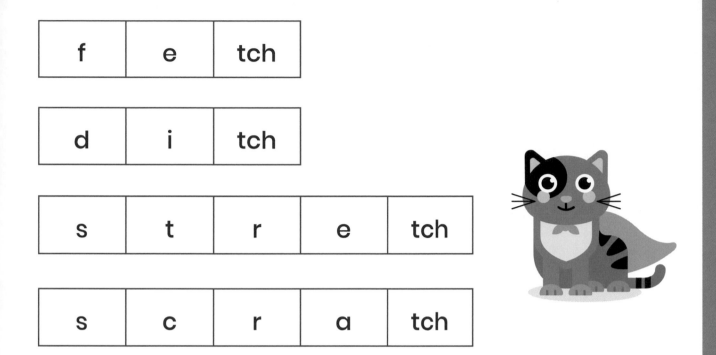

Write the words from above next to the correct picture.

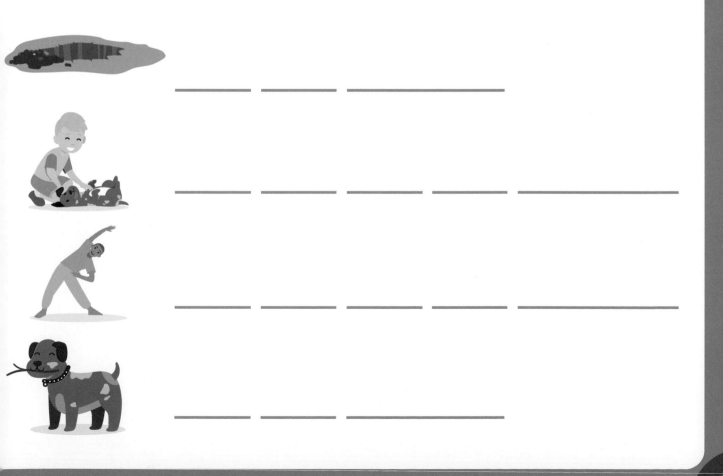

_____ _____ _____

_____ _____ _____ _____

_____ _____ _____

_____ _____

ve words

Read the words, then find them in the word search.

Check ✓ each word once you find it.

☐ give

☐ live

☐ solve

☐ valve

s	o	l	v	e
w	a	g	a	v
q	v	d	l	t
u	l	i	v	e
g	i	v	e	o

About Olive

Read about Olive.

I have   two legs and two wings.

I live   in my nest in the

big tree by the pond.

About me

Draw a picture of you.

Draw a picture of where you live.

Draw a picture of your pet or favorite animal.

Sounding out and blending: **ve** words

Blend the sounds in each square to read the whole word.

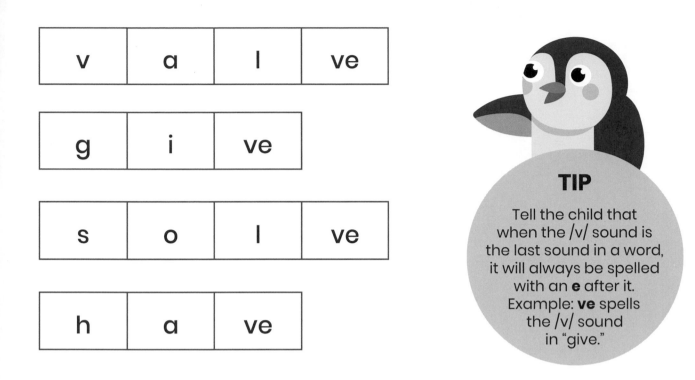

| v | a | l | ve |

| g | i | ve |

| s | o | l | ve |

| h | a | ve |

TIP

Tell the child that when the /v/ sound is the last sound in a word, it will always be spelled with an **e** after it. Example: **ve** spells the /v/ sound in "give."

Write the words from above next to the correct picture.

_____ _____ _____

_____ _____ _____

_____ _____ _____ _____

_____ _____ _____

Read the words in the box. Color the pictures that match the words in the box.

ditch	fetch	give	hatch
latch	Olive	scratch	witch

Segmenting words

Help Mitch the snake by filling in the missing **tch**.
Blend the sounds to read the whole word.

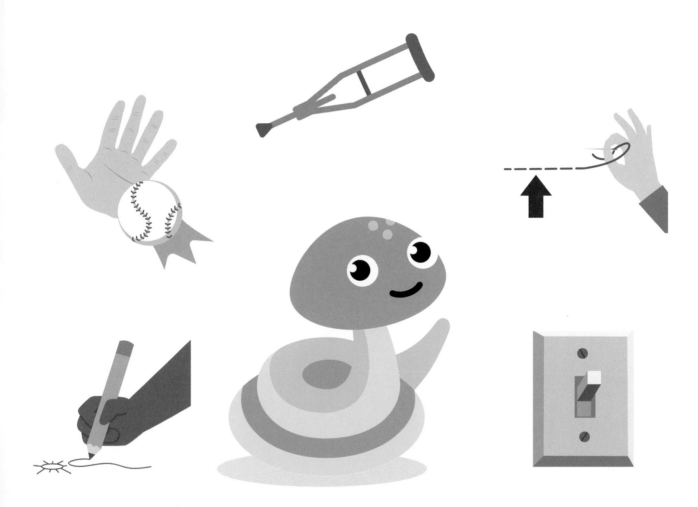

Mi _____

cru _____

ske _____

sti _____

ca _____

swi _____

Fill in the missing **ve**. Blend the sounds to read the whole word.

Sol _____ this!

Who left Oli _____ a gift?

Do they ha _____ legs?

Look at the picture and write the name of who you think left the gift.

Who was it? It was _____ !

Segmenting words

Fill in all the missing sounds. Blend the sounds to read the whole word.

Read the heart words.

talk

walk

could

Read the sentences. Match each sentence to the correct picture.

Sam and I talk a lot.

We walk to the match.

I could catch it!

Copy the heart words.

talk _____

walk _____

could _____

Write the heart words to complete the sentences.

I _____ to Bess at camp.

It was a long _____ to the match.

_____ you live in a den?

Read the sentences. Circle the correct word to complete each sentence.

The dog needs me to scratch the **itch / ditch** .

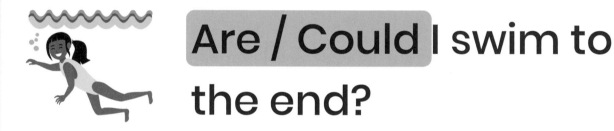

Are / Could I swim to the end?

Mitch does not **do / have** strong legs.

Read the story.

Olive and Mitch see a ditch.
Olive is up in a tree.

"I can stretch across that ditch.
I am strong," says Mitch.

Mitch stretches. Olive helps Mitch,
but she misses. Mitch stops in the ditch.

"Stretch across the ditch!" yells Olive.

"I will stick with it," says Mitch.

Olive hugs Mitch. "I knew you could do it!"
says Olive.

Draw your favorite part of the story.

Trace the sentence.

Olive and Mitch

see a ditch.

TIP

Before the child writes the sentence, dictate the sentence in phrases and have them say each word as they write. This helps build spelling skills by hearing the word and writing it.

Trace the sentence.

"I can stretch across

that ditch," says Mitch.

Trace the sentence.

"I will stick with it!"

says Mitch.

Trace the sentence.

"I knew you could

do it!"

Congratulations!

Now you know your **tch** and **ve** spellings.

Well done!

Collect an animal sticker to add to your journey map.

STAGE 6 COMPLETE

Have you collected all of your sound blend bubbles from the sticker page?

The three sounds of **ed**

The spelling of **ed** either sounds like /t/, /d/, or /id/.
Read the words in each column.

/t/	/d/	/id/
bumped	scanned	skidded
wished	drummed	panted
chopped	filled	patted
packed	rubbed	lifted

Circle the thing in each row that does not rhyme with the others.

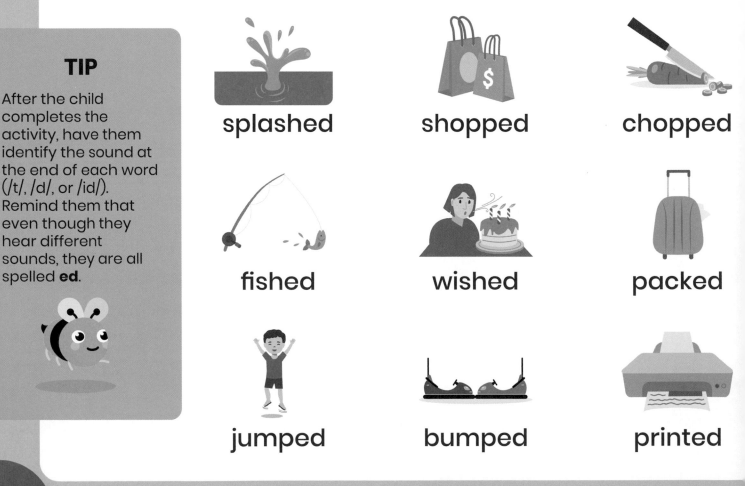

splashed   shopped   chopped

fished   wished   packed

jumped   bumped   printed

Sounding out and
blending: **ed** words

Blend the sounds in each square to read the whole word.

b	u	m	p	e	d

d	r	u	mm	e	d

p	a	tt	e	d

j	u	m	p	e	d

Write the words from above next to the correct picture.

_____ _____ _____ _____ _____ _____

_____ _____ _____ _____ _____ _____

_____ _____ _____ _____ _____ _____

_____ _____ _____ _____ _____ _____

Help Jared the bat by filling in the missing **ed** ending. All of the **ed** endings have the /t/ sound. Blend the sounds to read the whole word.

brush _____

kick _____

popp _____

fetch _____

skipp _____

Fill in all the missing sounds. Blend the sounds to read the whole word.

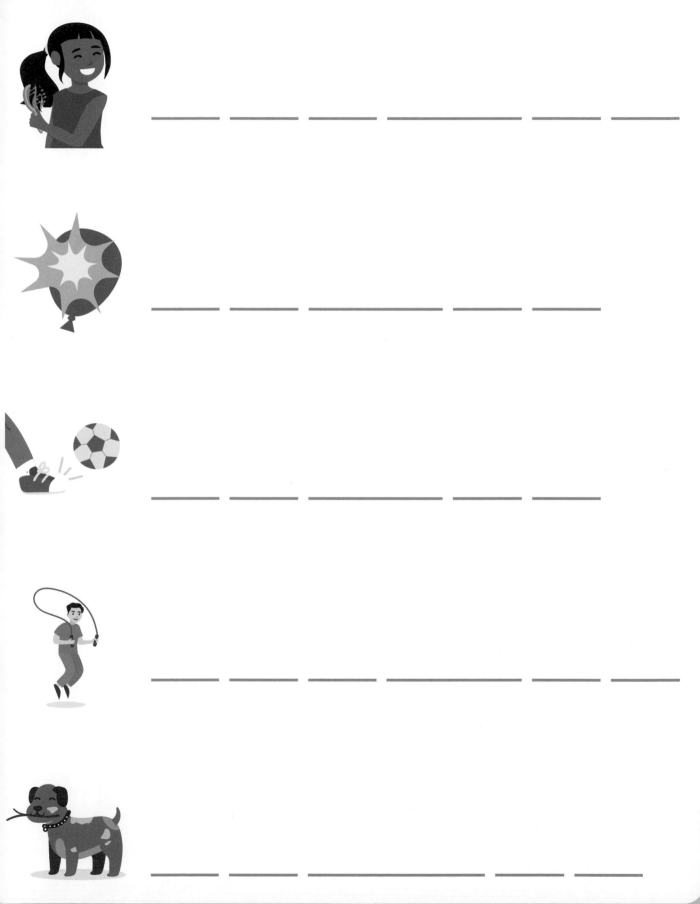

Read the heart words.

would

should

any

Read the sentences. Match each sentence with the correct picture.

We would not go.

She should stop drumming.

Are there any apples left?

Copy the heart words.

would _____

should _____

any _____

Write the heart words to complete the sentences.

Which one _____ you pick?

You _____ whisk the mix.

Are there _____ bottles on the shelf?

Read the sentences. Circle the correct word to complete each sentence.

 Is there **any / six** milk left?

 Two frogs **jumped / bumped** into the pond.

 Dan **patted / skipped** the cat.

Read the sentences. Find the sticker for each part of the story on the sticker page.

Quin checked her stash of fish. "No fish! This is bad!" she grunted.

Quin set a bag on the grass. She fished and dropped the fish into the bag.

Pam the cat sat in a tree. She hopped from the tree into the bag. She snacked on the fish.

When Quin picked up the bag, she was shocked. No fish, just a plump cat!

Trace the sentence.

Quin checked the
stash of fish.

Trace the sentence.

She fished and dropped
the fish into the bag.

Trace the sentence.

She hopped from
the tree.

Trace the sentence.

Quin picked up the bag.

Four-in-a-row game

For 1 to 4 players. You will need two sets of colored tokens. Take turns reading a word and putting a token on the word. The winner is the first to get four of their tokens in a row.

fished	would	chopped	spilled	cracked
rubbed	camped	filled	should	stopped
melted	drummed	chipped	landed	kicked
skilled	wished	patted	picked	handed
printed	dressed	rested	flicked	skidded
splashed	shocked	jumped	walked	hopped

ing words

Look at these words. Read each syllable and blend them together to read the whole word.

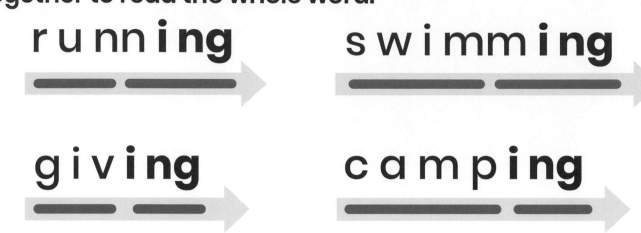

r u n n **i n g**

s w i m m **i n g**

g i v **i n g**

c a m p **i n g**

Look at these words and pictures. Say the words and match them with the pictures.

camping	running	scratching	giving

shopping	stitching	fishing	swimming

 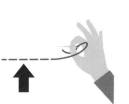 

Sounding out and blending: **ing** words

Blend the syllables in each rectangle to read the whole word.

drip	ping

pop	ping

fix	ing

dig	ging

TIP

When adding **ing** to base words, tell the child to double the consonant if the vowel sound is short. Example: "stop" > "stopping." If the base word has two consonant sounds, just add **ing**. Example: "mix" > "mixing."

Write the words from above next to the correct picture.

_____ _____

_____ _____

_____ _____

_____ _____

Segmenting words

Help Frank by filling in the missing **ing** ending. Blend the sounds to read the whole word.

yell _____

winn _____

whisk _____

juggl _____

hopp _____

Fill in all the missing syllables. Blend the syllables to read the whole word.

Read the heart words.

been

into

friend

Read the sentences. Match each sentence with the correct picture.

| I have been to the match. |

| Mitch jumps for his friend. |

| Do not go into the ditch! |

124

Copy the heart words.

been

into

friend

Write the heart words to complete the sentences.

Where have you _____ ?

Go _____ the hutch
to get an egg.

My _____ Ben can
sketch well.

Read the sentences. Circle the correct word to complete each sentence.

We have been / be on a trip.

We are walking / kicking to the top of that hill.

The bus is / are starting to move.

Read the sentences. Find the sticker for each part of the story on the sticker page.

It is hot. Quin and Lin are swimming.
Lin kicks and kicks.

Quin is running and jumping and she lands with a flop!
SPLASH!

"Where is my ring?"
Lin says, sobbing.

Quin swims to hunt for the ring. "It is lost!" Lin is upset. Then she sees the ring.

Writing sentences

Trace the sentence.

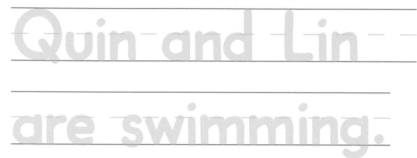

Quin and Lin
are swimming.

Trace the sentence.

Quin is running
and jumping.

Trace the sentence.

"Where is my ring?"
Lin says, sobbing.

Trace the sentence.

Quin is swimming.

Three-in-a-row game

For 2 players. You will need a die and some tokens. Take turns throwing the die. Read a word in that column and place your token on that word. The first player to have three tokens in a row in any direction is the winner!

swimming	drumming	clapping	stopping	blending	finishing
been	bragging	matching	dropping	snapping	spinning
shopping	boxing	sledding	wishing	fishing	into
flapping	friend	kicking	grinning	flopping	jumping
crunching	humming	stamping	snipping	yelling	flipping
selling	dripping	stitching	munching	grabbing	sticking

le words

Look at these words. Read each syllable and blend them together to read the whole word.

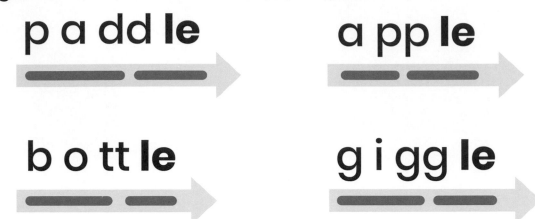

p a dd **le**

a pp **le**

b o tt **le**

g i gg **le**

Look at these words and pictures. Circle the two words that do not have a matching picture.

| apple | wiggle | candle | giggle |
| saddle | kettle | bottle | paddle |

Blend the syllables in each rectangle to read the whole word.

ket	tle

jug	gle

peb	ble

buck	le

TIP

Tell the child that the **le** will have a consonant right before it, and it makes the /ul/ sound. Example: the **ple** in "apple" makes the /pul/ sound, where the mouth is slightly open.

Write the words from above next to the correct picture.

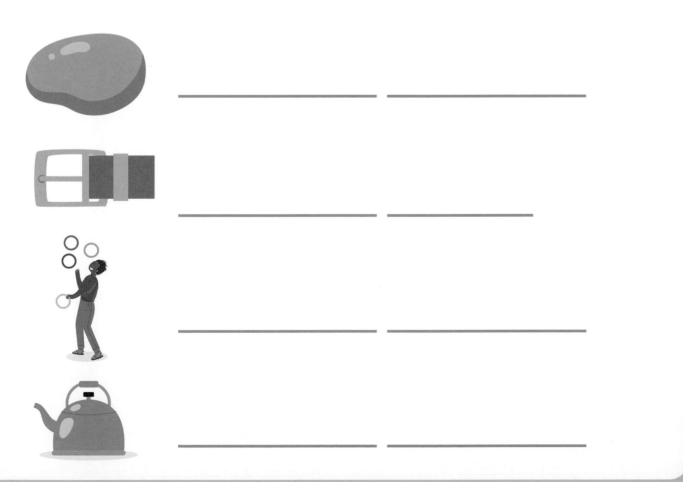

_____ _____

_____ _____

_____ _____

_____ _____

Help Bret by filling in the missing **le** ending. Blend the sounds to read the whole word.

bott _____   kett _____

hand _____   gigg _____

padd _____

Segmenting words

Fill in all the missing syllables. Blend the syllables to read the whole word.

Read the heart words.

because

four

fourth

Read the sentences. Match each sentence with the correct picture.

> I stitch the quilt because there is a rip.

> I skipped fast and was fourth!

> I jumped and got four in the net.

Copy the heart words.

because _____

four _____

fourth _____

Write the heart words to complete the sentences.

I switch on the lamp
_____ it is dark.

I planted _____ seeds.

She finished _____ .

Comprehension

Read the sentences. Circle the correct word to complete each sentence.

Jim **splashed / licked** the ice cream.

My dad **has / have** freckles.

There are **four / fourth** bottles in the bin.

Lin gives Bret a **cuddle / middle** .

TIP

After completing this activity, have the child create their own sentences with a word missing. Then have them quiz you! This helps them build their language skills.

Read the story.

Bell the bee was stuck in the middle of a web.

She stretched and wiggled. She was tangled up.

"Help!" Bell yelled. Just then, Jared flapped by. "What a muddle!" he said.

"Grab my little leg," said Jared. Bell held on and he pulled her free.

Draw your favorite part of the story.

Trace the sentence.

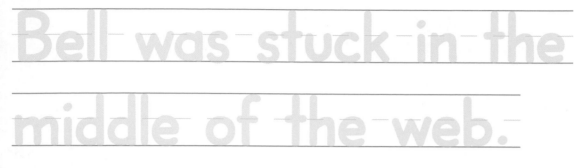

Bell was stuck in the middle of the web.

Trace the sentence.

She was tangled up.

Trace the sentence.

"What a muddle!"

Trace the sentence.

"Grab my little leg."

Congratulations!

Now you know your **ed**, **ing**, and **le** spellings.

Well done!

Collect an animal sticker to add to your journey map.

STAGE 7 COMPLETE

Have you collected all of your sound blend bubbles from the sticker page?

ed

le

ing

These two letters make the /ay/ sound.

a-e

Circle the things that have **a-e** in them.

TIP

Tell the child the /ay/ sound can be spelled with an **a** followed by a consonant and an **e**. The **a** and **e** work together so the **a** makes /a/ and the **e** does not make a sound.

Blend the sounds to read the word.

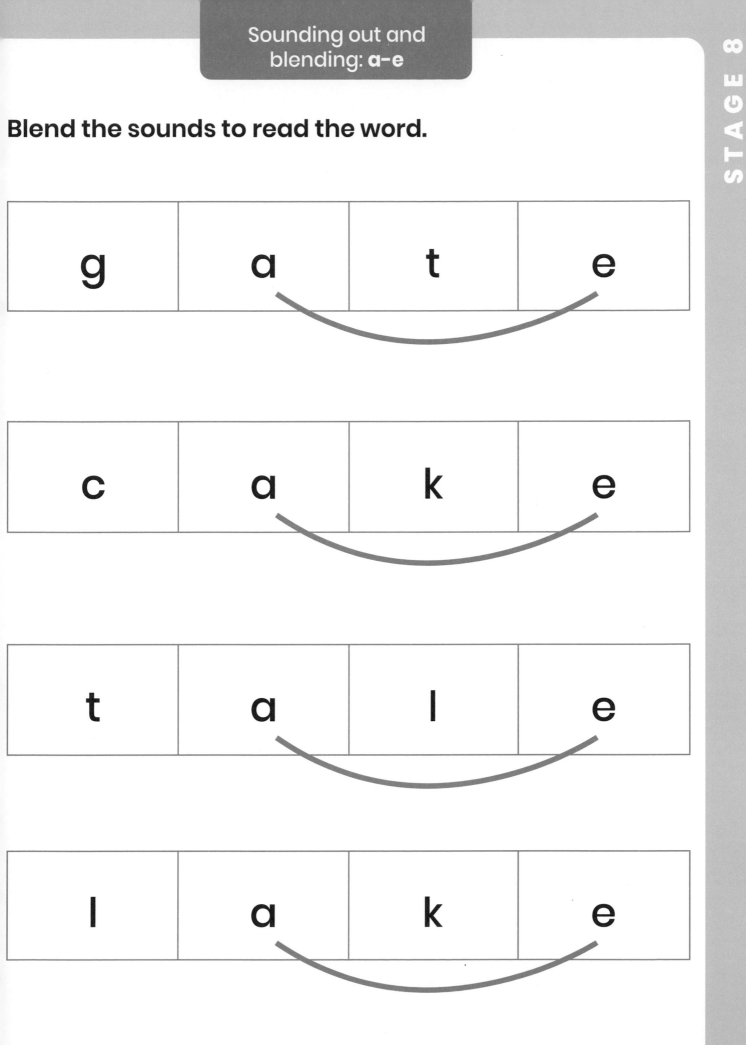

| g | a | t | e |

| c | a | k | e |

| t | a | l | e |

| l | a | k | e |

Fill in the sounds to spell the word. Draw a line to join the letters a-e. Blend the sounds to read the whole word.

g ___ t ___

c ___ k ___

p l ___ t ___

s n ___ k ___

Fill in all of the sounds to spell the word. Draw a line to join the letters **a-e**. Blend the sounds to read the whole word.

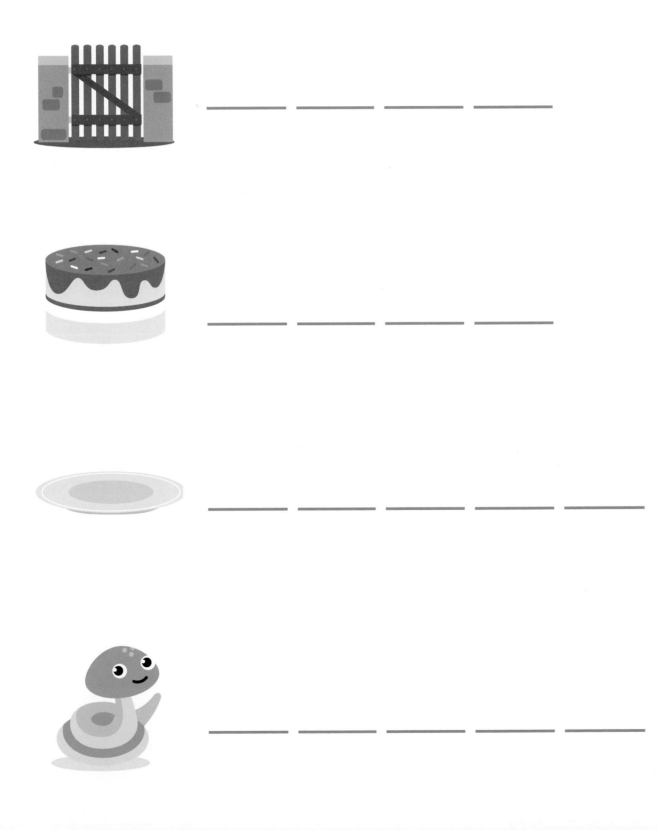

Read the heart words.

people

pretty

woman

Read the sentences. Match each sentence to the correct picture.

Some people have pet snakes.

I will bake a pretty cake.

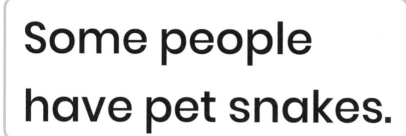

Jane is a woman.

Copy the heart words.

people _____

pretty _____

woman _____

Write the heart words to complete the sentences.

_____ tell tales of fate.

There is a _____ gate at the end of the lane.

The _____ is pale.

Read the sentences. Circle the correct word to complete each sentence.

 I will put it in a frame / flame .

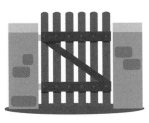 It was late so we shut the gaze / gate .

 Kate is the woman's name / tame .

 We went to a cake sale / brake .

Read the sentences. Match each part of the story to the correct picture

Jake, Fran, and Mitch the snake did a bake sale.

Jake was sad. People did not come for cakes.

Fran said, "The people will take it!"

They came for the cake!

Trace the sentence.

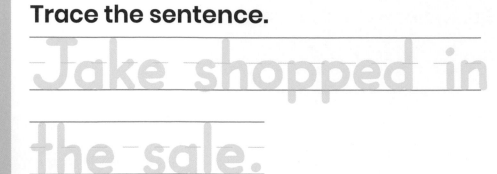

Jake shopped in
the sale.

Trace the sentence.

The woman went
on a plane.

Trace the sentence.

Lin has a red cape.

Trace the sentence.

People came for
the cake!

Jake's game

For 1 to 4 players. You will need tokens and a die. Take turns throwing the die and moving your token. Read the word you land on. If you land on a snake, you miss a turn. If you land on a ladder, go to the word at the top. The winner is the first person to the finish!

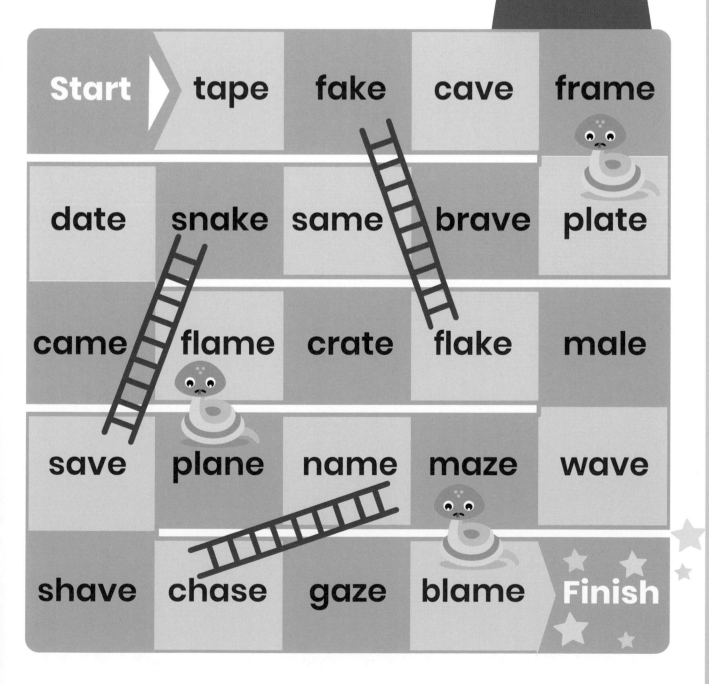

Start	tape	fake	cave	frame
date	snake	same	brave	plate
came	flame	crate	flake	male
save	plane	name	maze	wave
shave	chase	gaze	blame	Finish

Introducing e-e

These two letters make the /ee/ sound.

Check ✔ the things that have e-e in them.

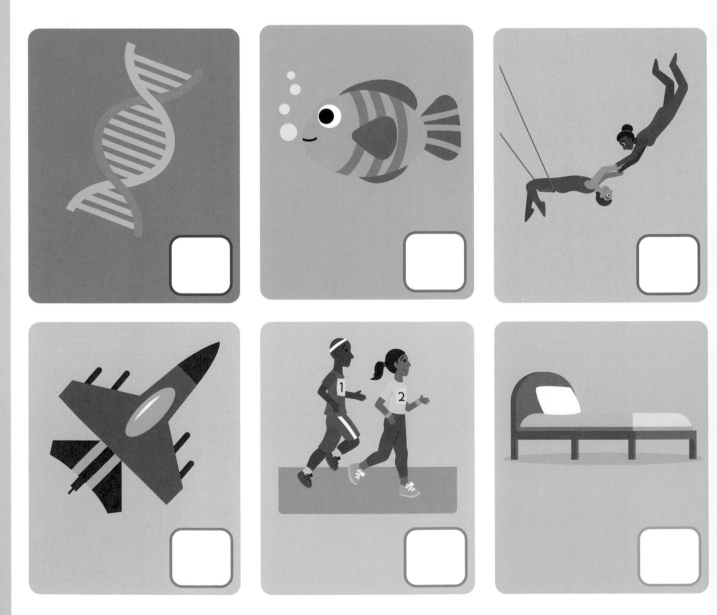

Blend the sounds to read the word.

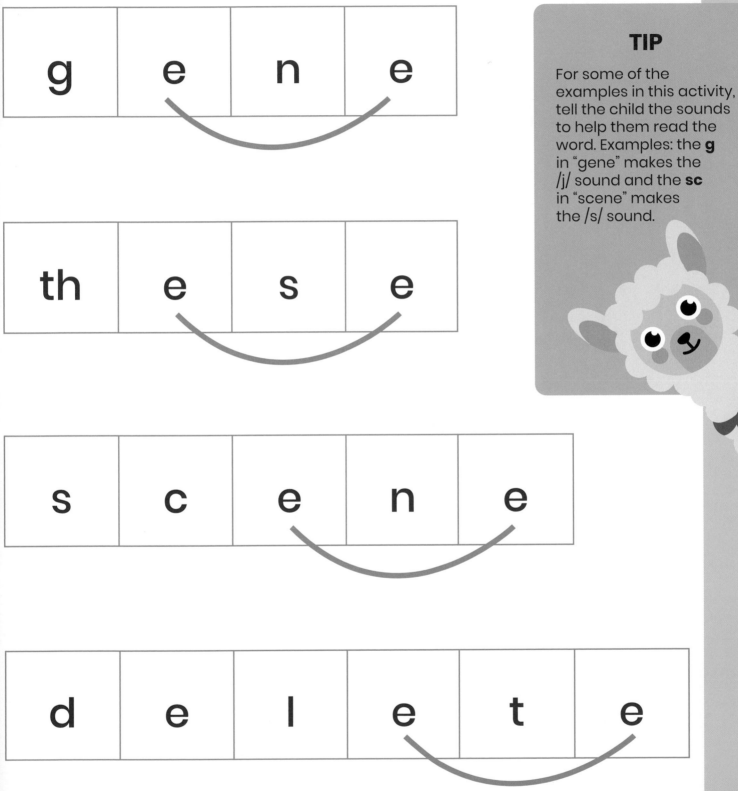

g	e	n	e

th	e	s	e

s	c	e	n	e

d	e	l	e	t	e

TIP

For some of the examples in this activity, tell the child the sounds to help them read the word. Examples: the **g** in "gene" makes the /j/ sound and the **sc** in "scene" makes the /s/ sound.

Fill in the sounds to spell the word. Draw a line to join the letters e-e. Blend the sounds to read the whole word.

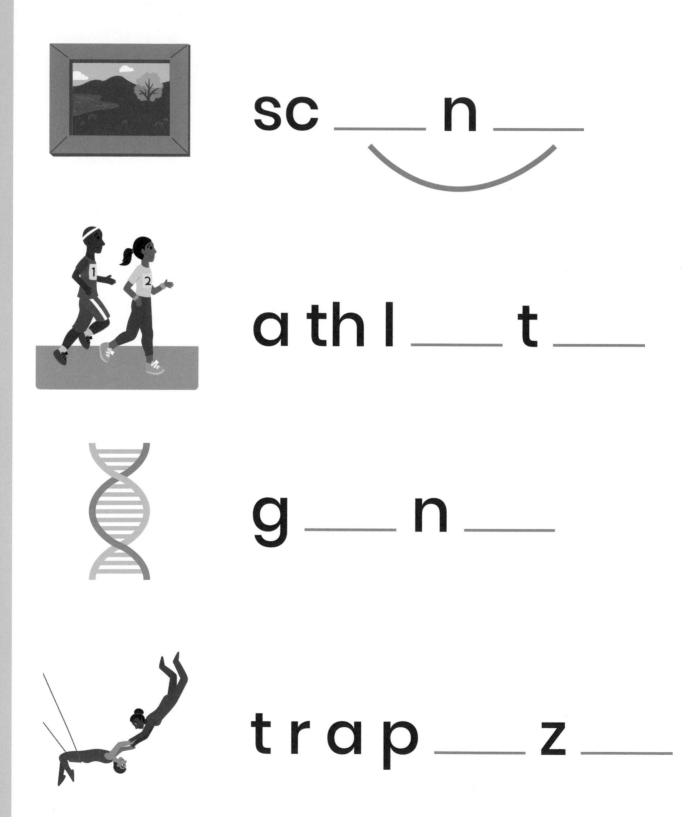

sc __ n __

a th l __ t __

g __ n __

t r a p __ z __

Fill in all of the sounds to spell the word. Draw a line to join the letters e–e. Blend the sounds to read the whole word.

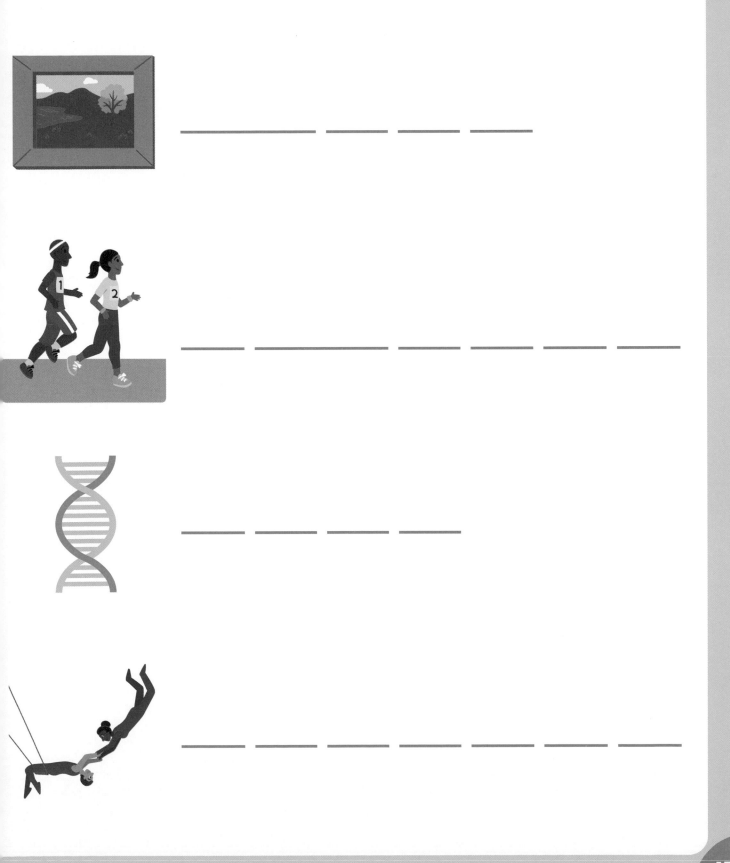

STAGE 8 : vowel consonant silent e

Read the heart words.

women
● ♥ ● ♥ ●

mo<u>v</u>e
● ♥ ●

bo<u>th</u>
● ♥ ●

Read the sentences. Match each sentence with the correct picture.

Jane and Eve are women.

Move these things!

Jake and Dave are both men.

154

Copy the heart words.

women

move

both

Write the heart words to complete the sentences.

The _____ swing

on the trapeze.

The athlete can

_____ fast.

Delete _____ of

these scenes.

Read the sentences. Circle the correct word to complete each sentence.

 There was a **stampede / serene** .

 The athletes will move fast and **compete / delete** to win.

 Both women will **complete / compete** the quiz.

 The winds were **extreme / theme** .

Tell a story

Read the sentences. Match each sentence to the correct picture.

Steve and Pete
will compete.

It is a stampede!
What a scene!

Pete is fast, but who
will be the top athlete?

The end! Steve and
Pete are both serene.

Trace the sentence.

This scene is a
complete mess!

Trace the sentence.

Will you press delete?

Trace the sentence.

The women have the
same genes.

Trace the sentence.

The lane is made
of concrete.

For 1 to 4 players. You will need two sets of colored tokens. Take turns to read each word and put a token on the word. The winner is the first to get four of their tokens in a row.

extreme	serene	complete	these
Steve	stampede	deplete	Eve
athlete	gene	concrete	delete
theme	Pete	compete	trapeze

These two letters make the /igh/ sound.

i-e

Color the things that have **i-e** in them.

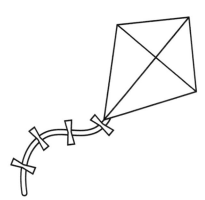

Sounding out and blending: **i-e**

Blend the sounds to read the word.

b	i	k	e

p	i	p	e

f	i	n	e

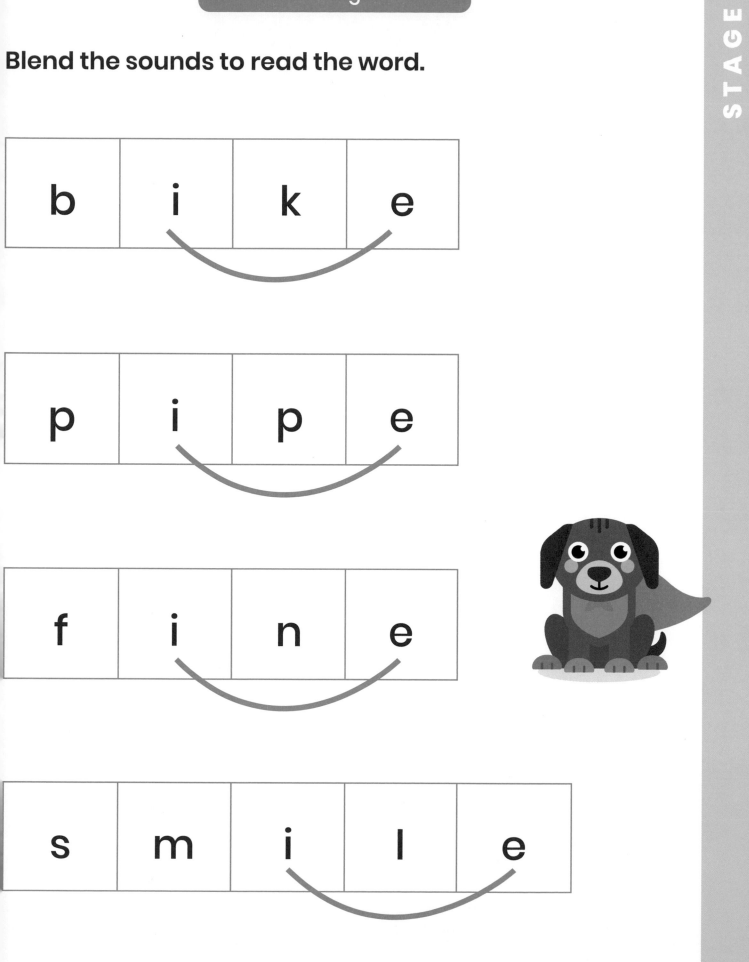

s	m	i	l	e

**Fill in the sounds to spell the word.
Draw a line to join the letters i-e.
Blend the sounds to read the
whole word.**

t ___ m ___

k ___ t ___

b ___ k ___

p r ___ z ___

Fill in all of the sounds to spell the word. Draw a line to join the letters **i-e**. Blend the sounds to read the whole word.

___ ___ ___ ___

___ ___ ___ ___

___ ___ ___ ___

___ ___ ___ ___ ___

Read the heart words.

nothing

other

another

Read the sentences. Match each sentence with the correct picture.

There was nothing for miles.	
Get the other bike.	
I would like another apple.	

Copy the heart words.

nothing _____

other _____

another _____

Write the heart words to complete the sentences.

There is _____ in the file.

Drive to the _____ street.

Do you have _____ kite?

Read the sentences. Circle the correct word to complete each sentence.

 What time / tame is it?

 The plane can glide / glad and dive.

 Your kite is red. Mine / Mile is green.

 The snake has nine stripes / slides .

Tell a story

Read the sentences. Match each part of the story to the correct picture.

Mike was awake on time.

He went to glide his kite at five.

Then he went for a dive at nine.

Mike had a big smile. Life was nothing but fun!

Trace the sentence.

Is a pine a tree?

Trace the sentence.

The flames in the fire
are hot.

Trace the sentence.

The mice ran up
the pipe.

Trace the sentence.

This lime is ripe, so
take another one.

Kite game

For 1 to 4 players. You will need tokens and a die. Take turns rolling the die and moving your token. Read the word you land on. If you land on a pipe, you miss a turn. If you land on a kite, take another turn. The winner is the first person to the sunshine.

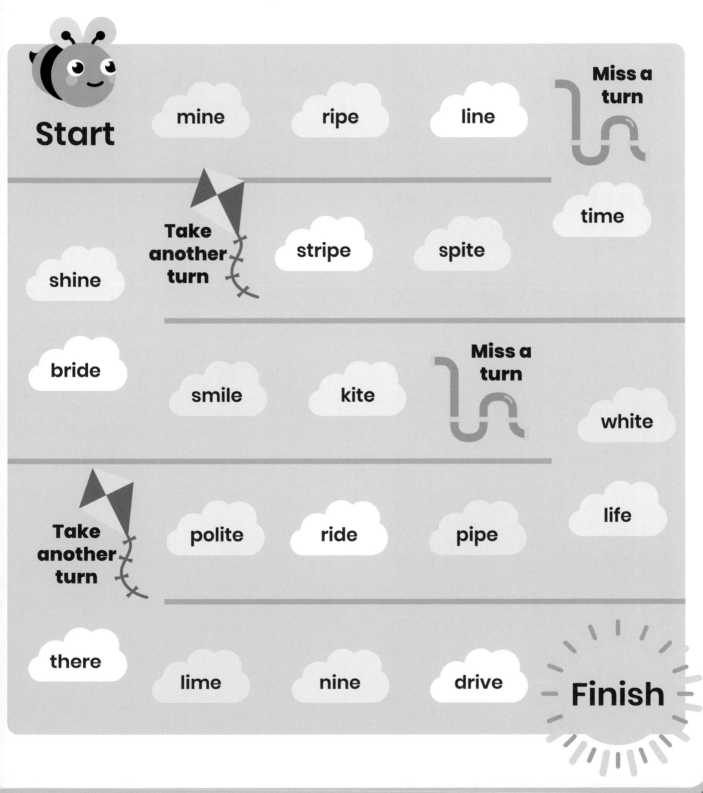

Start

mine · ripe · line · Miss a turn · time

Take another turn · stripe · spite

shine · bride · smile · kite · Miss a turn · white

Take another turn · polite · ride · pipe · life

there · lime · nine · drive · Finish

These two letters make the /oa/ sound.

Cross out the things that do not have **o-e** in them.

Blend the sounds to read the word.

b	o	n	e

p	o	l	e

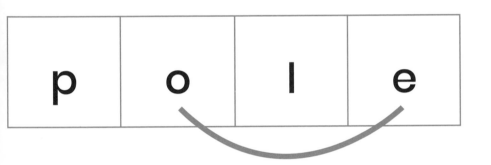

a	l	o	n	e

s	t	o	n	e

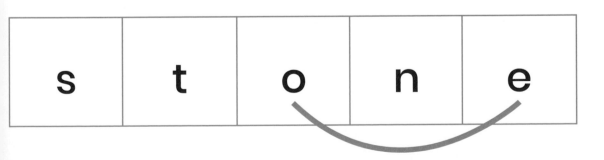

Fill in the sounds to spell the word. Draw a line to join the letters o-e. Blend the sounds to read the whole word.

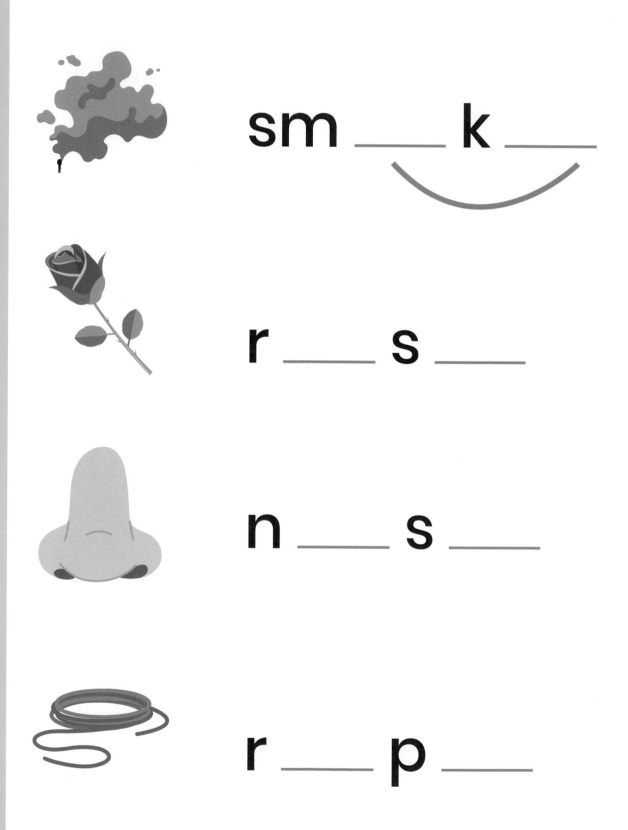

sm __ __ k __ __ __

r __ __ s __ __ __

n __ __ s __ __ __

r __ __ p __ __ __

Fill in all of the sounds to spell the word. Draw a line to join the letters o-e. Blend the sounds to read the whole word.

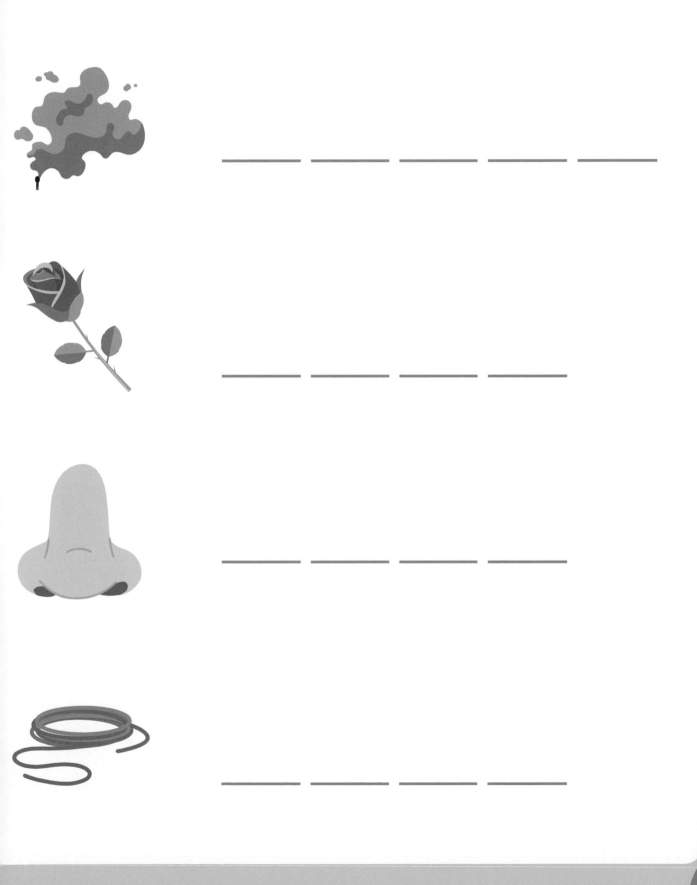

_____ _____ _____ _____ _____

_____ _____ _____ _____

_____ _____ _____ _____

_____ _____ _____ _____

Read the heart words.

mother

brother

today

Read the sentences. Match each sentence with the correct picture.

Mother drove home.

Her brother left a note.

Today, the pond froze.

Copy the heart words.

mother _____

brother _____

today _____

Write the heart words to complete the sentences.

My _____'s name
is Rose.

Her _____
broke a bone.

I went home late
_____ .

Read the sentences. Circle the correct word to complete each sentence.

I have a **globe / drove** at home.

My home is made of **stone / slope** .

I got back late so I left a **note / nose** .

There are lots of **broke / bones** in the spine.

Read the sentences. Match each sentence to the correct picture.

Today, Frank broke a bone.

He will sit and mope at home.

Jared tells a joke and Frank smiles.

They both drove to get a cone!

Trace the sentence.

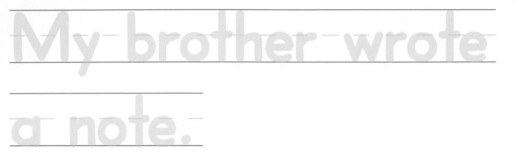

My brother wrote a note.

Trace the sentence.

I got a globe today.

Trace the sentence.

Delete the code!

Trace the sentence.

Mother spoke as we drove.

Four-in-a-row game

For 1 to 4 players. You will need two sets of colored tokens. Take turns reading a word and putting a token on the word. The winner is the first to get four of their tokens in a row. The winner places a token on one of the characters. The game is played four times until all the characters are covered.

globe	throne	home	drone	note
stone	vote	cone	hope	clone
dome	slope	bone	code	mope
spoke	tone	alone	quote	poke
zone	awoke	remote	froze	stroke

These two letters make the /oo/ sound.

Join the letters **u-e** to the things that have **u-e** in them.

u-e

Blend the sounds to read the word.

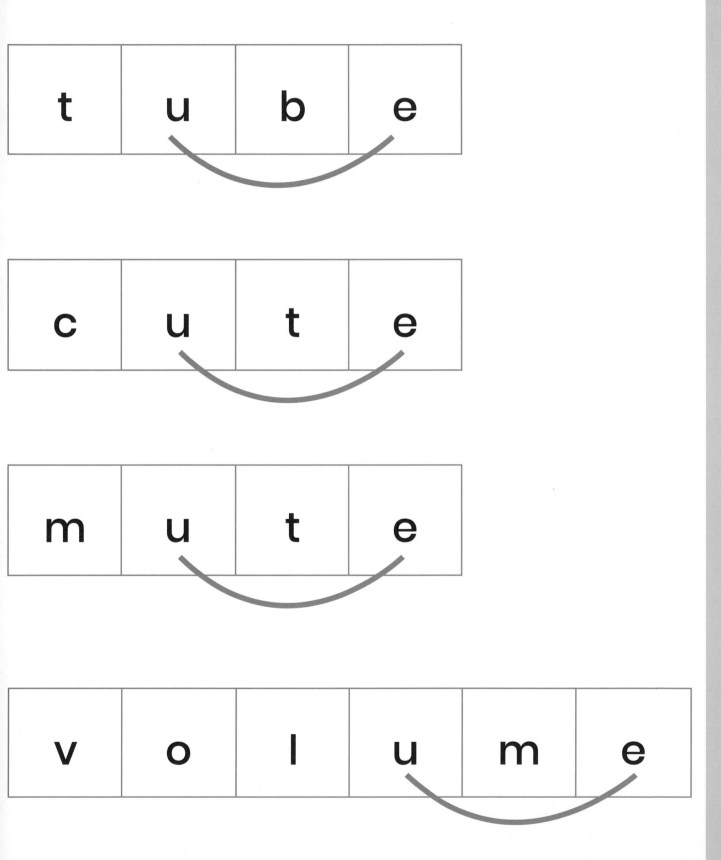

| t | u | b | e |

| c | u | t | e |

| m | u | t | e |

| v | o | l | u | m | e |

Segmenting **u-e**

Fill in the sounds to spell the word. Draw a line to join the letters u-e. Blend the sounds to read the whole word.

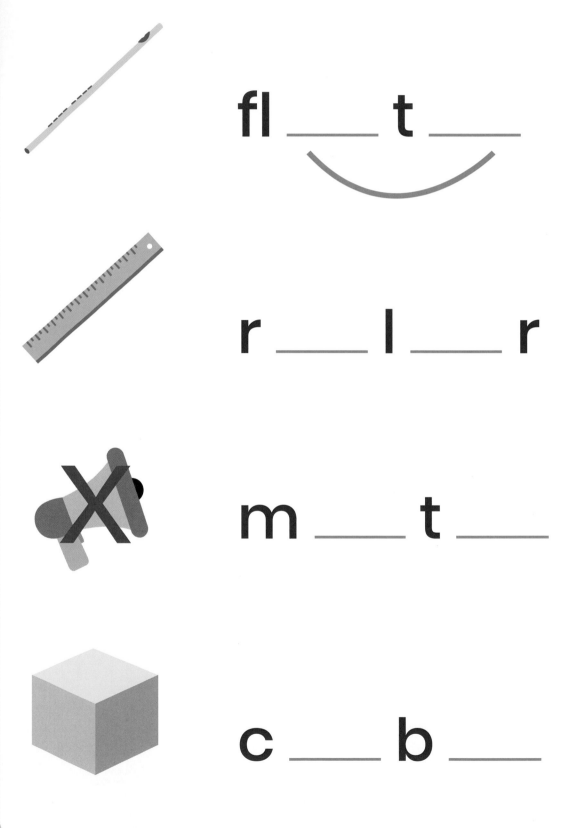

fl __ __ t __ __

r __ __ l __ __ r

m __ __ t __ __

c __ __ b __ __

Segmenting u-e

Fill in all of the sounds to spell the word. Draw a line to join the letters u-e. Blend the sounds to read the whole word.

_____ _____ _____ _____ _____

_____ _____ _____ _____ _____

_____ _____ _____ _____

_____ _____ _____ _____

Read the heart words.

very

above

among

Read the sentences. Match each sentence with the correct picture.

The kitten is very cute.

The huge tree is above me.

There was a ruler among the pens.

Copy the heart words.

very

above

among

Write the heart words to complete the sentences.

It can be _____
hot in June.

Put the ruler on the shelf
_____ .

There was a lute
_____ the flutes.

Read the sentences. Circle the correct word to complete each sentence.

A ruler / salute is very useful.

A flute can produce / reduce a tune.

Fumes can pollute / mute .

A cube / tube has six sides.

Read the sentences. Match each sentence to the correct picture.

Bell liked June.

She sang a sweet tune.

But Jim did not like the volume.

Don't intrude and be so rude, Jim!

Writing sentences

Trace the sentence.

Should I include rules?

Trace the sentence.

The volume is on mute.

Trace the sentence.

Do jokes amuse you?

Trace the sentence.

Flutes produce tunes.

TIP

Remind the child that words are written so they can be read. Have them create and write their own sentences using **u-e** words. Then read the sentences together!

Congratulations!

Now you know your
a-e, e-e, i-e, o-e
and **u-e** spellings.

Well done!

Collect an animal
sticker to add to
your journey map.

STAGE 8
COMPLETE

Have you collected all of
your sound blend bubbles
from the sticker page?

a-e   e-e   i-e

o-e   u-e

STAGE 1 : e e

Page 8

The following should be checked:
green, knee, sheep

Page 9

The following should be colored:
three, teeth, queen, cheese

Page 10

The following should be circled: sweep,
sheep, sneeze

Page 11

tree   seed   feed   beep

sleep   feet   see   bee

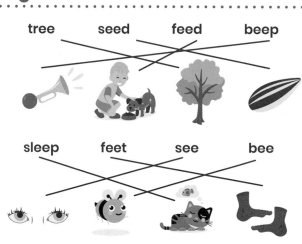

STAGE 2 : CVCC CCVC CCVCC

Pages 16–17

The following should be colored: bank, belt,
bugs, cats, cubs, gift, hand, jump, lamp, tent

Page 18

hand   gift   tent   bump

pink   milk   cats   lamp

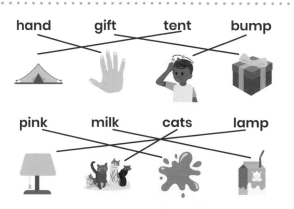

Page 19

cubs, belt, sand, jump

Page 20

bank, camp, wind, sink, bugs, hats

hats, bank, camp, sink, wind, bugs

Page 21

sink, camp, wind, bugs, hats, bank

sink, wind, bugs, hats, camp, bank

Page 22

The kids were
at camp.

Here is
a nest.

A cliff is
up there.

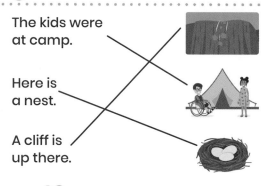

Page 23

The belt and the hats <u>were</u> left in the tent.

<u>Here</u> is the dent. Now the lamp is bent.

Where is the desk? It is <u>there</u>.

Page 24

The following words should be circled: pink,
tent, lamp

Page 25

Pages 28–29

The following should be checked: twig, plum,
clap, flag, flip, sled

Page 30

The following should be circled: clap, step

Page 31

sled, twig, grin, flag

Page 32

c<u>r</u>ab, d<u>r</u>um, s<u>w</u>im, s<u>k</u>ip, grin, s<u>l</u>ip

grin, s<u>w</u>im, s<u>k</u>ip, c<u>r</u>ab, s<u>l</u>ip, d<u>r</u>um

Page 33

c<u>r</u>ab, sk<u>i</u>p, sw<u>i</u>m, sl<u>i</u>p, dr<u>u</u>m, grin

slip, dru<u>m</u>, swi<u>m</u>, grin, skip, cra<u>b</u>

Page 34

Two cats slept on a mat.

He can jump up and flip.

She will skip and trip!

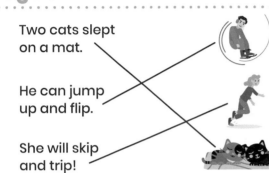

Page 35

What is one plus one? It is <u>two</u>.

Jen said <u>she</u> had a plan.

The man said <u>he</u> was lost.

Page 36

The following words should be circled: snap, glum, sled

Page 37

Fran the frog will sled and Bret the dog will run. Will Fran win? Will Bret win?

Fran's sled slid from the top of the hill. "I will win!" yells Fran.

Fran gets to the flag. "Huff! Puff!" says Bret.

Bret and Fran clap and grin. "It was so fun!"

Pages 40-41

All of the spots on the animals should be colored in.

A line should be drawn between the following: skunk and trunk

The following should be checked: plum

The following should be located in the word search and checked: print, spots, grunt, crept

Page 42

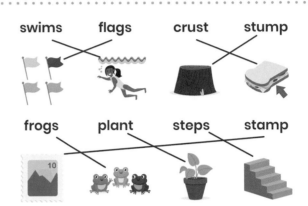

swims   flags   crust   stump

frogs   plant   steps   stamp

Page 43

drink, stunt, stomp, frost

Page 44

trunk, c<u>r</u>ust, s<u>t</u>omp, plant, t<u>w</u>igs, p<u>r</u>int

pl<u>a</u>nt, p<u>r</u>int, st<u>o</u>mp, t<u>w</u>igs, tr<u>u</u>nk, c<u>r</u>ust

Page 45

st<u>o</u>mp, twigs, tr<u>u</u>nk, pl<u>a</u>nt, pr<u>i</u>nt, cr<u>u</u>st

cru<u>s</u>t, twigs, prin<u>t</u>, plan<u>t</u>, trun<u>k</u>, sto<u>m</u>p

Page 46

We slept in a tent.

There will be frost on the twigs.

Tess yells to me.

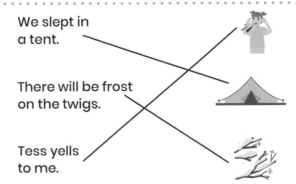

Page 47

Can a crab <u>be</u> a pet?

Mom tells <u>me</u> to get to bed.

<u>We</u> stop to rest and have a drink.

Page 48

The following should be circled: drank, me, be

STAGE 3 : ch sh th

Page 52

The following should be circled: lunchbox, pinch

Page 53

cheek, lunch, chat, chop

Page 54

Page 55

shed, wish, ship, shelf

Page 56

The following should be colored: moth, sloth

Page 57

think, three, fifth, cloth

Page 58

The following should be checked: sloth, moth, chicken, fish, splash, shed, sheep, lunch

Page 59

The sections containing the following should be colored: shelf, cloth, fish, throne, chick, shorts

Page 60

b<u>e</u>nch, <u>ch</u>imp, <u>sh</u>elf, <u>b</u>rush, fif<u>th</u>, <u>s</u>ixth

b<u>r</u>ush, s<u>i</u>xth, ch<u>i</u>mp, f<u>i</u>fth, b<u>e</u>nch, sh<u>e</u>lf

Page 61

sh<u>e</u>lf, s<u>i</u>xth, b<u>e</u>nch, ch<u>i</u>mp, f<u>i</u>fth, br<u>u</u>sh

fif<u>th</u>, bru<u>sh</u>, shel<u>f</u>, ben<u>ch</u>, chim<u>p</u>, six<u>th</u>

Page 62

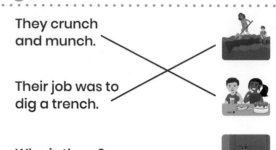

They crunch and munch.

Their job was to dig a trench.

Who is there?

Page 63

<u>They</u> are chums.

The twins lost <u>their</u> lunchbox.

<u>Who</u> let that cat in?

Page 64

The following should be circled: their, sixth, Thank

Page 65

The chimp should be colored.

The following should be circled: sloth, moth, cloth

STAGE 4 : ck ng

Page 68

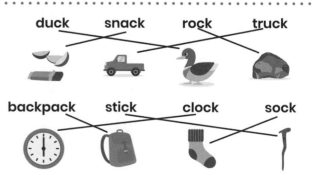

duck   snack   rock   truck

backpack   stick   clock   sock

Page 69

shock, luck, trick, sack

Page 70

The following should be circled: long, strong

Page 71

string, things, long, bang

Page 72

The following should be checked: clock, backpack, chick, lock, sock

Page 73

The sections containing the following should be colored: sock, backpack, chick, clock, lock

Page 74

s̲ting, w̲ings, c̲ling, r̲ocks, l̲icks, t̲rick

t̲rick, l̲icks, w̲ings, c̲ling, s̲ting, r̲ocks

Page 75

wi̲ngs, tri̲ck, ro̲cks, li̲cks, sti̲ng, cli̲ng

cli̲ng, li̲cks, wi̲ngs, tri̲ck, ro̲cks, sti̲ng

Page 76

My socks are red.

The ducks are by the pond.

You and I sing songs.

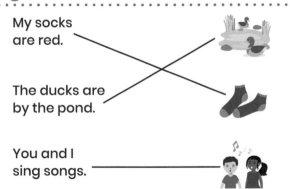

Page 77

<u>My</u> dad had a long trip.

The swings are <u>by</u> the shed.

Can <u>you</u> bring snacks?

Page 78

The following should be circled: my, pack, thick

Page 79

"When can I get on the swing?" says Frank.

"You can get on at six," says Jim.

Tick, Tock. It is ten. Frank is mad and bangs the swing.

"Bad luck, Frank!" says Jim. "Let's get back to the camp."

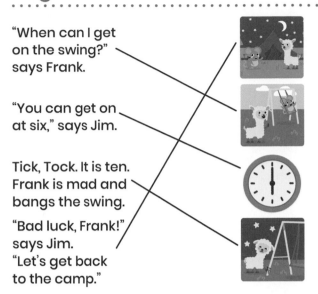

STAGE 5 : qu wh

Page 82

The queen should be colored in.

Quin the penguin should be colored in.

The cheetah should be circled.

Page 83

quick, queen, Quin, quiz

Page 84

The following should be checked: whistle, whisper, whale

Page 85

whisk, wheel, whiff, whack

Page 86

A line should be drawn through the following words: queen, quick, quest, quiz, quit

Page 84

The clouds containing the following should be colored: whack, wheel, which, whip

Page 88

<u>qu</u> a c k, <u>qu</u> ee n, <u>Qu</u> i n, <u>qu</u> i l t

Page 89

<u>wh</u> i s k, <u>wh</u> i ff, <u>wh</u> ee l

Page 90

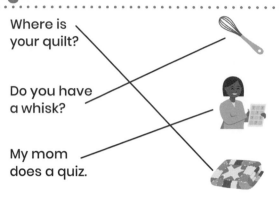

Where is your quilt?

Do you have a whisk?

My mom does a quiz.

Page 91

<u>Your</u> wheel is flat.

Can you <u>do</u> a quick trick?

What <u>does</u> a queen do?

Page 92

The following should be circled: Does, your, quick

Page 93

"Where is Lin?" asks Fran.

"Which path should I hop up?" asks Fran.

"Here I am. Quick! I will get up the hill!" says Lin.

"I win! I am the queen of the hill!" says Fran.

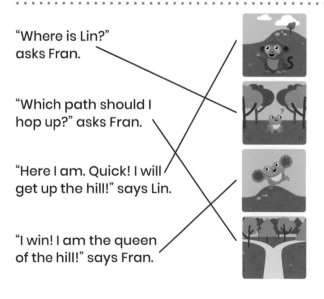

STAGE 6 : t c h v e

Page 96

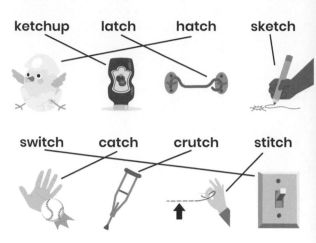

ketchup   latch   hatch   sketch

switch   catch   crutch   stitch

Page 97

ditch, scratch, stretch, fetch

Page 98

The following should be checked: give, live, solve, valve

Page 99

have, give, solve, valve

Page 100

The following should be colored: ditch, fetch, give, hatch, latch, Olive, scratch, witch

Page 101

Mi <u>tch</u>, c r u <u>tch</u>, s k e <u>tch</u>, s t i <u>tch</u>, c a <u>tch</u>, s w i <u>tch</u>

Page 102

Sol<u>ve</u> this!

Who left Ol<u>ive</u> a gift?

Do they ha<u>ve</u> legs?

Who was it? It was <u>Mitch</u>!

Page 103

solve, Mitch, give, Olive, catch, fetch

Page 104

Sam and I talk a lot.

We walk to the match.

I could catch it!

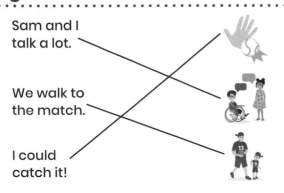

Page 105

I <u>talk</u> to Bess at camp.

It was a long <u>walk</u> to the pitch.

<u>Could</u> you live in a den?

Page 106

The following should be circled: itch, Could, have

STAGE 7 : ed ing le

Page 110

The following should be circled: splashed, packed, printed

Page 111

patted, bumped, jumped, drummed

Page 112

br u sh <u>ed</u>, k i ck <u>ed</u>, p o pp <u>ed</u>, f e tch <u>ed</u>, s k i pp <u>ed</u>

Page 113

brushed, popped, kicked, skipped, fetched

Page 114

We would not go.

She should stop drumming.

Are there any apples left?

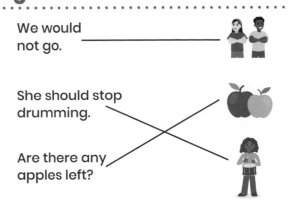

Page 115

Which one <u>would</u> you pick?

You <u>should</u> whisk the mix.

Are there <u>any</u> bottles on the shelf?

Page 116

The following should be circled: any, jumped, patted

Page 117

Page 120

camping   running   scratching   giving

shopping   stitching   fishing   swimming

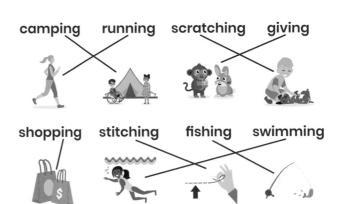

Page 121

popping, dripping, digging, fixing

Page 122

y e ll <u>ing</u>, w i nn <u>ing</u>, wh i s k <u>ing</u>, j u gg l <u>ing</u>, h o pp <u>ing</u>

Page 123

yelling, whisking, hopping, juggling, winning

Page 124

I have been to the match.

Mitch jumps for his friend.

Do not go into the ditch!

Page 125

Where have you <u>been</u>?

Go <u>into</u> the hutch to get an egg.

My <u>friend</u> Ben can sketch well.

Page 126

The following should be circled: been, walking, is

Page 127

Page 130

The following should be circled: wiggle, saddle

Page 131

pebble, buckle, juggle, kettle

Page 132

bott<u>le</u>, kett<u>le</u>, hand<u>le</u>, gigg<u>le</u>, padd<u>le</u>

Page 133

bottle, kettle, handle, paddle, giggle

Page 134

I stitch the quilt because there is a rip.

I skipped fast and was fourth!

I jumped and got four in the net.

Page 135

I switch on the lamp <u>because</u> it is dark.

I planted <u>four</u> seeds.

She finished <u>fourth</u>.

Page 136

The following should be circled: licked, has, four, cuddle

STAGE 8 : V C silent e

Page 140

The following should be circled: plane, cake, game, plate

Page 142

g<u>a</u>t<u>e</u>, c<u>a</u>k<u>e</u>, pl<u>a</u>t<u>e</u>, sn<u>a</u>k<u>e</u>

Page 143

gate, cake, plate, snake

Page 144

Some people have pet snakes.

I will bake a pretty cake.

Jane is a woman.

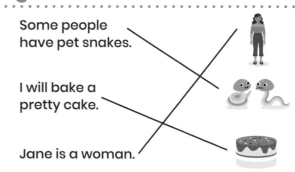

Page 145

<u>People</u> tell tales of fate.

There is a <u>pretty</u> gate at the end of the lane.

The <u>woman</u> is pale.

Page 146

The following should be circled: frame, gate, name, sale

Page 147

Jake, Fran, and Mitch the snake did a bake sale.

Jake was sad. People did not come for cakes.

Fran said, "The people will take it!"

They came for the cake!

Page 150

The following should be checked: gene, trapeze, athlete

Page 152

sc<u>e</u>ne, <u>a</u>thl<u>e</u>t<u>e</u>, g<u>e</u>n<u>e</u>, tr<u>a</u>p<u>e</u>z<u>e</u>

Page 153

scene, athlete, gene, trapeze

Page 154

Jane and Eve are women.

Move these things!

Jake and Dave are both men.

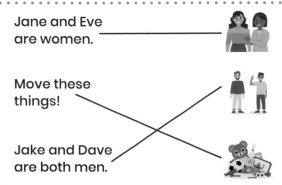

Page 155

The <u>women</u> swing on the trapeze.

The athlete can <u>move</u> fast.

Delete <u>both</u> of these scenes.

Page 156

The following should be circled: stampede, compete, complete, extreme

Page 157

Steve and Pete will compete.

It is a stampede! What a scene!

Pete is fast, but who will be the top athlete?

The end! Steve and Pete are both serene.

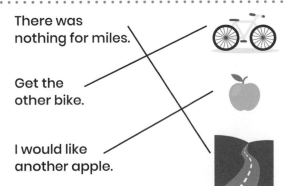

Page 160

The following should be colored: kite, bike, fire, slide

Page 162

t<u>i</u>m<u>e</u>, k<u>i</u>t<u>e</u>, b<u>i</u>k<u>e</u>, pr<u>i</u>z<u>e</u>

Page 163

time, kite, bike, prize

Page 164

There was nothing for miles.

Get the other bike.

I would like another apple.

Page 165

There is <u>nothing</u> in the file.

Drive to the <u>other</u> street.

Do you have <u>another</u> kite?

Page 166

The following should be circled: time, glide, Mine, stripes

Page 167

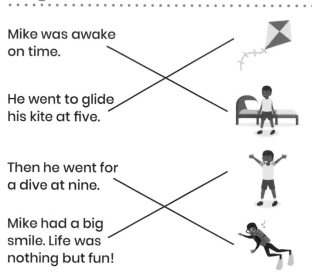

Mike was awake on time.

He went to glide his kite at five.

Then he went for a dive at nine.

Mike had a big smile. Life was nothing but fun!

Page 170

The following should be crossed out: lemon, umbrella, sun, windmill

Page 172

sm<u>o</u>ke, r<u>o</u>se, n<u>o</u>se, r<u>o</u>pe

Page 173

smoke, rose, nose, rope

Page 174

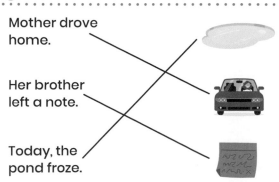

Mother drove home.

Her brother left a note.

Today, the pond froze.

Page 175

My <u>mother</u>'s name is Rose.

Her <u>brother</u> broke a bone.

I went home late <u>today</u>.

Page 176

The following should be circled: globe, stone, note, bones

Page 177

Today, Frank broke a bone.

He will sit and mope at home.

Jared tells a joke and Frank smiles.

They both drove to get a cone!

Page 180

The following should have lines drawn to them: cube, tube, flute

Page 182

fl<u>u</u>te, r<u>u</u>ler, m<u>u</u>te, c<u>u</u>be

Page 183

flute, ruler, mute, cube

Page 184

The kitten is very cute.

The huge tree is above me.

There was a ruler among the pens.

Page 185

It can be <u>very</u> hot in June.

Use a ruler to put a line <u>above</u>.

There was a lute <u>among</u> the flutes.

Page 186

The following words should be circled: ruler, produce, pollute, cube

Page 187

Bell liked June.

She sang a sweet tune.

But Jim did not like the volume.

Don't intrude and be so rude, Jim!

Congratulations!

You completed the book!

Sound Blends STAR

Well done!

Now you know all of your sound blends.

Collect the sound blends star to complete your journey map.